# California
# Eden

# California Eden

## Heritage Landscapes of the Golden State

Christine Edstrom O'Hara
and Susan Chamberlin

Opposite: Fan palms frame a view of the Mesquite Golf Course and Country Club in Palm Springs, which is undergoing restoration as a desert environment named the Prescott Preserve. Overleaf: There are enough roses introduced by California nurseries to fill a book. The red and white-striped climbing rose on the left is 'Fourth of July,' bred by Tom Carruth. Overleaf, Next: Perkins Park, a vernacular landscape on the bluffs of Pacific Grove, overlooks Monterey Bay.

For Bill Grant and David Streatfield
With thanks to all the people who
created these cultural landscapes

Opposite: Ornamental grasses such as this giant feather grass (*Celtica*, formerly *Stipa gigantea*) have been popular since pampas grass was introduced to California in the mid-nineteenth century. Overleaf 1: This contemporary garden, "Sunnylands" in Palm Springs, uses succulents in masses, not as individual specimens, a style that may have originated at Ganna Walsaka's Lotusland. Overleaf 2: The pool at Val Verde, designed by Lockwood de Forest, Jr.

# INTRODUCTION

Christine Edstrom O'Hara
and Susan Chamberlin

**T**here are many untold stories in our built environment. *California Eden* looks at history through the lens of cultural landscapes—landscapes that have been shaped by humans who have left their imprints on the natural world. The story begins with the state's unique endemic flora, which evolved due to its isolation from the rest of the continent. There is a rich horticultural history dating back to its Indigenous communities. Indigenous Californians were not simply hunter-gatherers in an untouched wilderness. They practiced landscape management techniques defined by anthropologists as protoagriculture (not quite full domestication) and prescribed burn pyrodiversity (producing a landscape mosaic of enhanced food and other resources[1]). In addition to burning, a few horticultural techniques were employed, such as coppicing plants to promote straight shoots for basketmaking and cordage.

Today's diverse cultural landscapes have roots in the late eighteenth-century Spanish colonization of what was then called Alta California, the territory north of Baja California. Indigenous people were displaced from their ancestral lands by Europeans, and diseases reduced their numbers, a process that accelerated during the gold rush and statehood in 1850. Those who survived were forced onto reservations.[2] Early settlers transformed the landscape, sometimes inadvertently, through the introduction of invasive plant species, fire suppression, cattle ranching, golf courses, wetland draining, seawalls, water projects, and the eradication of grizzly bears, wolves, and elk.

Introduced plants, including palm trees grown at the missions for Palm Sunday services, olive trees harvested for olive oil, and the exotic (to eastern eyes) figs and oranges, all helped create an image of a Garden of Eden in the minds of California's visitors during the nineteenth century.[3] Some returned to settle and establish their own orange orchards sheltered by windbreaks of fast-growing, non-native blue

Above Left: Indigenous Californians with harpoons in a reed canoe in the San Francisco Bay around 1815. To renew their supply of tule reeds, some communities burned them, a type of landscape management. Above Right: Cattle grazing in spring on invasive, annual grasses, both originally introduced by the Spanish. Hundreds of years of grazing the hillside, combined with a natural process called terracette, produced the parallel furrows visible on the slopes below the oak trees. Opposite: A wildflower superbloom of native California poppies and chia in the Lake Elsinore area, an example of California's unique endemic flora.

  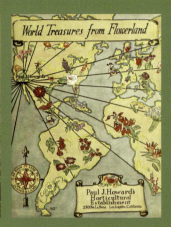

gum eucalyptus trees. By the end of the nineteenth century, the average California garden had forms inspired by Victorian gardens on the East Coast and in England but full of imported, exotic plants. It seemed that if enough water was applied, anything would grow in the benign Mediterranean climate (categorized as one of only a few such Mediterranean climates in the world).[4]

Coming from arid climates in Spain and Mexico, the Spanish colonizers considered water a precious resource. They created water projects at the missions based on systems engineered by the ancient Romans and Moors. Aqueducts delivered water for irrigating crops and to community fountains. The dam built by the Indigenous Chumash people in 1807 for Mission Santa Barbara still exists in the foothills above the mission, as does much of the infrastructure. Water was channeled by gravity to two reservoirs, as well as to a grist mill, a filter house, a fountain in front of the mission, and then to a large laundry basin before the wash water was finally emptied into the fields. During the subsequent American period, water was privatized and exploited. Some water rights date back to the gold rush era. By the twentieth century, massive dams, reservoirs, pumping stations, diversions, and canals delivered water over long distances to permit population growth, ranching, golf courses, and farming in areas where that might not otherwise be possible.

For many new settlers, California offered freedom from the accepted norms of the long-established eastern part of the country, as well as Europe. This was sometimes reflected in unusual landscape designs and the extraordinary array of plant material choices. The first California nurseries were established in Sacramento and in the Bay Area in the mid-nineteenth century. Blue gum eucalyptus (*Eucalyptus globulus*) arrived as seed from Australia at Walker's Golden Gate Nursery in 1859, and was quickly adopted in the state for timber and windbreaks.[5] While blue gums proved to be unsuitable for timber, many useful and ornamental eucalyptus species are still popular. Nobody introduced more plants to the state than Dr. Francesco Franceschi. He liked native plants, but one of his goals was to have something in bloom in every month of the year.

Other California nurserymen and women, as well as ordinary citizens, have introduced trees, shrubs, and flowers from all over the world. They have also introduced beloved plants that were their own creations through breeding or the selection of superior, natural variations. The seedless Washington navel orange, which the Portuguese sent to their colony, Brazil, was first grown in California by Mrs. L.C.

Above Left: Oranges were introduced by the Spanish colonizers to Alta California, but it was the settlers after the gold rush who transformed the Southern California landscape with orchards of citrus, which were shipped in boxes labeled with Edenic images. Above Center: The artist Henry Chapman Ford depicted his unique Victorian cottage and garden in Carpinteria with the numerous exotic plants he collected. Above Right: This early twentieth-century catalog cover illustrates the origins of numerous non-native plants imported and propagated by nurseries to beautify California gardens. Opposite: The sweetheart rose vine, 'Climbing Cécile Brünner', was introduced by Franz Hosp of Riverside in 1894. Overleaf: The California Aqueduct, seen here in the San Joaquin Valley, is one of many projects that delivers water long distances to farms, ranches, and urban areas.

(Eliza) Tibbetts in Riverside County, then introduced to the United States through the Department of Agriculture in 1875. Theodosia E. Shepherd in Ventura was noted for the petunias, nasturtiums, and cosmos she began hybridizing in the mid-1880s. Alfred D. Robinson bred some of the finest-known begonias, some from seed he obtained from Shepherd. E.O. Orpet was famous for his *Aeonium* succulents from North Africa and the Mediterranean region. Franz Hosp of Riverside gave us the vining sweetheart rose ('Climbing Cécile Brünner') in 1894, which he discovered as a sport of the dwarf polyantha 'Cécile Brünner' shrub rose. This climber can be found in gardens throughout the country. 'Queen Elizabeth,' perhaps the most famous rose of all, was hybridized by Dr. Walter E. Lammerts of Los Angeles. (Details for all the award-winning California roses could take up this entire book.)

Plant introductions continue to this day throughout California, but some things have proved to be tenacious or invasive—Mexican feather grass (*Nassella tenuissima*) is a recent example among the many ornamental grasses that have spread their seed on the wind and now threaten the environment, including pampas grass (*Cortaderia selloana*), which has invaded the Big Sur region, and fountain grass (*Pennisetum setaceum*), which has invaded the natural palm oasis in Anza-Borrego Desert State Park.

Perhaps the most unique example of an exotic California garden is Lotusland in Montecito. The property was originally the nursery of R. Kinton Stevens. In the 1920s, it was transformed into the

Below: Lotusland in Montecito is one of the most exotic and surrealistic gardens in California, if not the world. Opposite: Non-native fountain grass has invaded the native California fan palm oasis in Anza-Borrego Desert State Park.

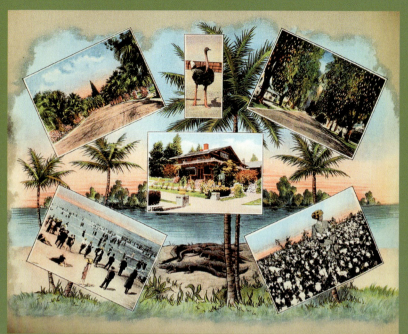 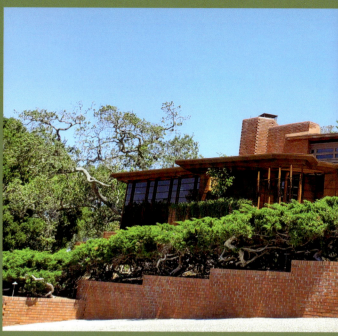

formally designed Cuesta Linda estate, then was renamed and remodeled by Madame Ganna Walska from 1941 to 1984. Beginning with the help of Lockwood de Forest Jr. and later with assistance from Ralph T. Stevens and numerous other landscape architects and horticulturists, Walska created a surrealistic wonderland that would become influential worldwide when Lotusland opened as a public botanical garden in 1993.[6]

In some ways, Lotusland is a typical garden because, like most California gardens, it features plants that originated elsewhere. While generations of native plant enthusiasts have bred or selected outstanding examples of ceanothus, Pacific Coast iris (*Iris douglasiana*), coral bells (*Heuchera*), monkeyflower (*Mimulus*), penstemon, sage (*Salvia*), and lupine, native plants have only recently received the widespread attention they deserve because they are usually very resilient in drought situations. People who think of palm trees as imports from tropical climates are surprised to learn that there is a drought-tolerant palm tree native to California. *Washingtonia filifera*, or the California fan palm, is found in the desert regions of the southwestern part of the state where water is near the surface or occurs in springs—Palm Springs being the most famous example of a natural palm oasis. It became a fashionable resort city in the early 1900s. However, as local water and imported supplies are diminishing, irrigating golf courses, lawns, and farms in the desert is no longer considered sustainable.

Landscape history has often focused on grand estate gardens designed by landscape architects, but less grand gardens are equally worthy of study. In the 1950s, the insightful cultural geographer J.B. Jackson inspired research into vernacular landscapes, which drew appreciation to everyday places that have evolved over time by the people whose activities shaped them.[7]

Cultural landscapes are broadly defined in this book as any outdoor space in the built environment. The book's organization is both thematic and chronological, with essays representing a range of landscape types, time periods, and geographic areas within the state. *California Eden* highlights little-known narratives: from the vernacular transformation of Sonoma County in a succession of grazing, logging, and the propagation of new plants to a military installation on the California-Mexico border, where First Lady Pat Nixon dedicated a park and expressed America's friendship for the Mexican people; and from the Cypress Lawn Memorial Park in Colma, a nineteenth-century metaphorical garden for the dead and its living visitors, to Frank Lloyd Wright's Hanna House and garden on the Stanford University campus,

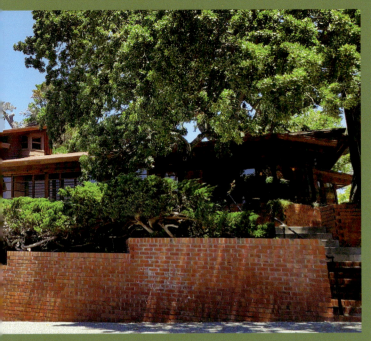 

where his theories of organic architecture were expressed in both house and landscape.

While landscape history has associations with architectural history, scholars of architecture tend to focus on the building while treating the landscape as its setting. Often overlooked, however, is the value and importance of the landscape on its own terms. Landscape design, like architecture, is a cultural construct. It is the product of working with a site's specific ecology, its sunlight, slopes, climate, and soils, but also its cultural and economic contexts. For example, the elaborate estate gardens developed in Northern California on the San Francisco Peninsula during the late nineteenth century reflected the influence of extreme wealth derived initially from the 1849 gold rush that transformed the region into the state's financial hub, while in Southern California, wealthy people from the East Coast and Midwest built their lavish estates to escape the winter months back home. In the 1920s, gardens throughout the state featured a highly romanticized version of the original rustic and utilitarian colonial gardens, appropriating Spanish culture to lend regional identity and beauty to American cities on the West Coast.

The concept of beauty meanwhile is in constant flux. Like other design fields, such as fashion and art in which aesthetics change as culture changes, each historic period for landscape design eschewed the styles of the past. Victorian-era gardens with exotic plants bordering winding paths or featuring clipped topiaries and carpet bedding gave way to more architectonic gardens with thoughtful planting during the great estate era of the late nineteenth and early twentieth centuries and then to naturalistic designs. Beginning in the Depression years, the preference was for modernist creations with minimalism driving geometric and biomorphic layouts and plant choices. In the postmodern period, it was not unusual for California landscape architects to incorporate symbolism into forms and spaces. Gardens now increasingly feature native plants and address sustainability issues. In contrast to gardens laid out by those educated in the principles of design, vernacular landscapes that evolved over time with various layers of use might have no intentional design at all.

Design and its history are catching up with the times. Recent scholarship has begun to address

Above Left: Meant to entice people to Los Angeles, the images on the back cover of this promotional booklet printed around 1914, represent vernacular landscapes. Above Center: Hanna House and its gardens were designed by Frank Lloyd Wright in association with his clients. Above Right: This Spanish Colonial Revival-style garden with romanticized plantings was painted by Colin Campbell Cooper around 1920.

> *"Gardens are metaphysical symbols of the relationship between human society and Nature. Gardens can be great works of High art, works of vernacular art, they can also be places associated with ceremony, embody power, and order. They can heal, inspire, and be places of production and serve a considerable array of practical purposes. In short, they are among human society's greatest creative achievements."[8]*

—David C. Streatfield, from an address to the second founding meeting of the California Garden & Landscape History Society in 1996

vernacular landscapes and gardens created by people of color. These places were previously little valued because their designers often were excluded from educational programs and professional publications. Kendall H. Brown has written extensively about Japanese-style gardens on the West Coast. During the past twenty years, Black leaders in landscape architecture, such as Walter J. Hood, have developed projects for communities or to highlight historical events that have been ignored. Other designers have begun to address and celebrate the role of Indigenous people at sites such as Tongva Park in Santa Monica.

Whether professionally designed or vernacular, historical context informs our understanding of a landscape within its specific setting and time. Studying landscape history is a way to understand the shaping of spaces in the environment as well as their meaning and our culture's values in a given period of time at a given site. There are surprising histories and little-known places for readers to discover in *California Eden*. This book begins to fill the gaps in our landscape history by including the story of Japanese Americans interned during World War II who lost their farms, gardens, and freedom; the role of women in horticulture and landscape architecture; and topics such as shopping malls, streetscapes, world fairs, and cemeteries. We hope the need to preserve these ephemeral places will be clear.

Above Left: El Novillero, the Donnell estate in Sonoma County, has a garden designed by Thomas D. Church in 1948, which is now recognized as a masterpiece of mid-century modernism. Above Right: Some structures in Tongva Park in Santa Monica were inspired by the traditional dwellings of the Indigenous Tongva people. Opposite: Sites in California discussed in this book.

Grass Valley

Sonoma

San Francisco
Colma

Danville

Oakland

Palo Alto &
Woodside

Santa Cruz

Monterey

Fresno

Santa Barbara

Pasadena & San Marino

Los Angeles

Palos Verdes

Anza Borrego

Border Field Park

# PART 1
# EXTRAORDINARY PLACES THE WORK OF LANDSCAPE ARCHITECTS AND DESIGNERS

California's landscape architects and designers are visionaries who give form to the extraordinary places illustrated in this section. Formal garden design was common in the late nineteenth century for grand estates, while the naturalistic style, derived from English Picturesque landscape painting, was preferred for parks and informal properties stuffed with exotic plants. At the turn of the century, design theories evolved as the concept of regionalism arose, which led to a new awareness about an appropriate aesthetic for coastal California's mainly Mediterranean climate and Spanish colonial past.

Working in most of California meant reckoning with a winter-wet, summer-dry landscape and limited water availability. As the landscape architect Lockwood de Forest Jr. noted, irrigated green lawns juxtaposed with California's golden summer hillsides looked like a can of paint had been spilled. The plant palette developed for the West Coast's challenges helped ground later modernist designs in this region after modernism, which originated in Europe, swept the United States.

The San Francisco Peninsula, extending south from the city of San Francisco to the Santa Clara Valley, was the site of extravagant estates constructed during the late nineteenth to early twentieth century for wealthy people who desired to escape the notorious summer fog that plagued them in their mansions in San Francisco. On the peninsula in Woodside, Agnes and William Bowers Bourn Jr. built their summer home, Filoli, in 1917. Here, sixteen acres of formal gardens were sited within more than six hundred acres of woodlands near Crystal Springs Reservoir. The Bourns' other summer home, a "cottage" surrounded by lush formal gardens next to William's gold mine in Grass Valley, was begun twenty years earlier. Beginning in about 1911, the Fleishhacker family built their summer home, Green Gables, in Woodside, employing one of the best architects of the time, Charles Sumner Greene, of the premier Arts and Crafts–era Pasadena-based firm, Greene and Greene, to design both the buildings and the landscape. Meanwhile, in Southern California, winter homes were constructed for affluent people who wanted to escape harsh eastern winters.

Landscape historian David Streatfield observed that during the 1920s, the theory emerged from the Arts and Crafts movement that architecture and landscape design in California should reflect and be rooted in the region. He also noted that the Japanese concept of borrowed scenery could link a garden to its region by incorporating the colors and materials from distant views into a site.[1] A few forward-thinking designers applied these principles and traditions from vernacular and local conditions, or from Mediterranean regions with climates similar to the West Coast, to produce new styles. Perhaps the first was Boston-based Frederick Law Olmsted Sr. A major designer of New York's Central Park, he developed regionally inspired landscapes in California at Stanford University and Mountain View Cemetery.

*"Almost everyone is familiar with the advertisement showing the world in the process of being covered with paint. The same effect results when lawns are spilled indiscriminately over our California hillsides."*

—Lockwood de Forest Jr., "Do Lawns Belong in Southern California?," 1924

Native plants, and in Southern California, drought-tolerant plants, were embraced as a way to express regionalism and conserve water instead of using the exotic plants of the past. Landscape architects who found their inspiration in local conditions were the Olmsted Brothers, who had taken over their father's firm in Boston, and Lockwood de Forest Jr. of Santa Barbara. Frederick Law Olmsted Jr. and James "Fred" Dawson, a partner in Olmsted Brothers, both relocated to California in the 1920s to develop the affluent community of Palos Verdes in an early example of sustainable landscape design on the West Coast. In Santa Barbara, de Forest developed numerous regionally inspired gardens and pioneered the use of borrowed scenery. Also, in association with Ervanna Bowen Bissell (and later Beatrix Farrand), de Forest laid out the Santa Barbara Botanic Garden in ecological communities, developing the first botanical garden in California devoted exclusively to native plants.

The architect Frank Lloyd Wright is known for his exceptional regional statement: Fallingwater in Pennsylvania, where stones from the site and a waterfall are incorporated into the architecture. Designed at about the same time in Palo Alto, Wright's 1937 Hanna House on the Stanford University campus was a seamless integration of indoor and outdoor space nestled into the hills and existing native oaks. Also located within existing native oak trees that same year across the San Francisco Bay from Palo Alto was the new home and garden of playwright Eugene O'Neill and his wife Carlotta. However, their isolation and failure to grasp the limitations imposed by the dry climate on their garden and new orchards would prove frustrating.

In addition to a regional approach to building and landscape architecture in California, the early twentieth century included another cultural shift: women landscape designers entered the profession. Landscape design was one of few vocations acceptable for women, because anything to do with gardens was considered domestic in nature. Landscape architect Beatrix Farrand is a striking anomaly as the only woman in 1899 among the eleven founding members of the American Society of Landscape Architects and as a designer of college campuses. Her example would pave the way for women landscape architects, including Katherine Bashford and Ruth Shellhorn, who were able to expand beyond residential design to much more encompassing portfolios of work. They would add to the rich tapestry of extraordinary places in California.

Overleaf: The formal gardens at Filoli in Woodside were laid out by landscape designer Bruce Porter between 1917 and 1922, with plantings and color schemes designed by horticulturist Isabella Worn.

# THE EMPIRE COTTAGE IN GRASS VALLEY
## WILLIAM BOWERS BOURN JR., WILLIS POLK, AND OSCAR PRAGER

Phoebe Cutler

Between 1897 and 1906 in the Sierra Nevada foothill town of Grass Valley, William Bowers Bourn Jr. launched a garden that, over a span of more than a century and against all normal expectations, has matured into a glorious old age. Located 130 miles northeast of San Francisco, Grass Valley and nearby Nevada City were dusty, scrappy towns surrounded by bare hills denuded of trees by the insatiable demand of the gold rush and the subsequent mining industry. It was an unlikely environment to find not only a distinguished house and garden but also a graduate of Cambridge University and his New York bride. Nevertheless, William Bowers Bourn Jr. acquired the Empire Mine in 1879, five years after returning from Britain, following the premature death of his father. (Bourn Sr. had controlled the mine in the early 1870s. His son took majority ownership over the course of two different periods, from 1879 to 1888 and from 1896 to 1929.) It was during the second period that the San Francisco native revived and modernized the mine operation. With equal perspicacity and even more determination, Bourn, supported by his wife, Agnes Moody Bourn, matched two disparate but able professionals who, under their guidance, created a sylvan compound of country home, recreation facility, and two additional staff houses.

The setting itself, despite being at an elevation of three thousand feet, with lovely, distant mountain views, would have thrown off most would-be garden makers because the most daunting factor was the identity of the nearest neighbor. Within a few hundred feet sat a hardrock gold mine. This, the Empire Mine, established in 1850 under another name, would prove to be arguably the largest and most prolific gold mine in California over the course of its one-hundred-year life, but the inherent blasting, drilling, crushing, and refining did not make it a choice backdrop for the showplace estate of a wealthy family.

The Bourn's Empire Cottage was designed by Willis Polk as an English manor-style house using brick and waste rock from the nearby mine.

Finding able professionals was essential, because simultaneously with assembling this oasis, Bourn was building a utilities empire: a gas-and-electricity monopoly (the forerunner of the modern behemoth Pacific Gas and Electric) followed in turn by an even more noncompetitive business that supplied water to the San Francisco Bay Area via the Hetch Hetchy Aqueduct. For the ambitious complex of the Empire Cottage main house, two ancillary ones, and the "clubhouse" recreation facility, architect Willis Jefferson Polk was the logical choice. Talented and experienced, he had just completed "Will" and Agnes's Pacific Heights mansion in San Francisco in 1897.

We may never know how Bourn located Oscar Albert Prager, a German immigrant with rudimentary English newly arrived on the West Coast, to design the garden. Bourn was fortunate to find him. At this early date in Northern California's garden history, Prager's credentials were difficult to rival. Not only had he graduated from the prestigious Royal Academy of Gardening in Potsdam, but the Leipzig native had

Above: The Empire Mine's hard rock miners from Cornwall, England toiled in a vast underground network that extended from the depths below Bourn Cottage to the rock underlying the city of Grass Valley. Left: The Empire Mine complex, now a State Park that includes the cottage, begins several hundred feet from the cottage's formal landscape.

also worked at Muskau Park, Prince Pückler-Muskau's legendary estate on the modern border between Germany and Poland. This extant historic domain is considered the continent's largest and most renowned example of eighteenth-century English-style landscape design. Discovering Prager allowed Bourn to complete the team that would undertake the task of developing an unusual business and recreational complex in the raw backcountry of the Sierra foothills.

Will Bourn would likely have worked closely with his architect on the house's siting because later sources described him assiduously scouring the property that would become Filoli in Woodside, the mansion that preempted the Empire Cottage. Before construction could begin in Grass Valley, access to the cottage had to be planned. The garden site was thirteen acres centered on a gentle rise. A private carriage drive off the encompassing public road (East Empire Street) was prepared to the rear, or northeast side, of the house site at the top of the slope. This arrangement optimized open space for both planting and vistas, especially the mountain views to the southwest.

Correspondence and an early photo suggest that the Bourns did not wait long after the house was up to begin a garden. A letter, written by an employee and relative, indicates the existence as early as 1903 of a "lovely ground about the house all beautifully kept with the loveliest roses and plants comparing favorably with some of the places in Tuxedo" (the exclusive, late nineteenth-century enclave north of New York City).[1] An early photo of the east side of the cottage shows a crude, winding path bordered on one side by indistinct low planting and on the other by scattered young trees. Even if Polk had been available for advice at this time, gardens and plants were not his forté. As it was, between 1901 and 1903, Polk was working for Daniel Burnham in Chicago. For his part, Prager, by the fall of 1901, had only just arrived on the West Coast, too late to take responsibility for a Tuxedo Park–worthy landscape less than two years later. Indeed, the combination of the letter and photo indicates that any early efforts probably relied on a local gardener and nursery.

In fact, the Bourns themselves might not have been monitoring these elementary efforts, because between 1901 and 1903, they made extensive trips abroad. On the second of their two trips, specifically to Switzerland and Italy, they discovered the Italian villa garden. In 1903, Agnes rhapsodized about the "beautiful and rare trees" of a garden near Bellagio in northern Italy, declaring its grounds and planting "the most beautiful things I have ever seen."[2] It is not inconceivable to imagine that, upon their return from these trips, they found the grounds of the Empire Cottage lacking, in which case they would have been thrilled to discover the availability in the San Francisco Bay Area of a highly trained landscape architect steeped in formal European garden traditions.

By 1903, the Italian villa garden had begun its long ascendance on the coasts of the US as the epito-me of the modern garden. Prager, schooled in Frederick II's mid-eighteenth-century palace gardens in Potsdam and guided by his own travels in Italy, was well situated to offer the San Francisco couple the fashionable garden they now realized they required. His plan, when completed, highlighted that consummate sixteenth-century Italian Renaissance feature: the cascade. The classical principles of geometry, symmetry, and vertical perspective dominated from the triple-tiered cutting and vegetable garden on the back, or approach side, to the central cascade's water chain and its geometric reflecting pool on the opposite, or southwest side. Except for the extension of the entry road, the paths are uniformly rectilinear. A large rectangular walk bounds the upper lawn in front of the house and connects it with the reflecting pool.

Three maple allées furthered the continental theme. Bordering the top of the rectangular walk, matching double rows of five red maples (*Acer rubrum*) extended from either side of the house. The "Main Avenue"—labeled "Maple Lane" on modern plans— became the third and major allée. Consisting of Norway maples (*A. platanoides*), it ran the whole bottom of the garden, beginning at the encircling East Empire

Below: An early view of the east side of the Bourn cottage, about 1900, shows that initial efforts to install a garden coincided with the building of the main house and preceded Prager's plan. Opposite: The clubhouse in the southwest corner of the grounds offered tennis and squash for the entertainment of the Bourn family, their guests, and mine superintendents—but not the miners. Overleaf: To please the Bourns, Oscar Prager designed the landscape based on Italian villa gardens. They are now maintained by volunteers and state park staff.

Street, skirting the reflecting pool, and ending at the clubhouse in the southeast corner. An archival photo shows this allée, formerly the dirt path used by the miners to reach the mine yard, turfed and sumptuously lined by shrubs and floral borders, the eponymous maples not yet visible. To accommodate the workers, a new entrance was created at the east side of the yard, an arrangement that did not solve any noise problems but at least offered some visual distance from the source of much of the Bourns' prosperity.

Prager's preliminary "scetch" (*sic*) called for multiple small to medium groves. A numbering system keyed to a lost legend called for twenty-five different trees or shrubs. Three handwritten insertions ("Populus Carolina," "Lombardy poplar," and "birches") on the preserved blueprint give some idea of the species the landscape architect had in mind. One of the largest stands filled the southwest interior of the large rectangular walk. The grove bordered the cascade and cov-

*Above: The northeast side of the house has a picturesque rose arbor and steps that descend to the cutting garden. Opposite: The cascade, or water chain, required massing the ground behind it into a grass terrace. Willis Polk's ornate retaining walls improved upon Prager's original design.*

ered much of the rise from the avenue to the fountain wall at the top of the water chain. The effect would have been very different from the existing situation of a sunny expanse of turf punctuated by four stately Italian cypress trees (*Cupressus sempervirens*).

Presumably, the Bourns requested a reforestation to restore screening as well as a canopy to the denuded site. Polk seems to have gone further. His 1905 plan, "Garden and Grounds of the Empire Cottage & Club," the second, more finished of two reworkings of Prager's landscaping, specifies "forest" in four places. This landscape vision of the pre-mining era incorporated a woodland that began across Main Avenue's grass walk and covered the hillside from the clubhouse on the east to an equal distance on the west. The dense plantation would have advanced on both sides of the cascade and overlapped into the open lawn area in front of the cottage. Four narrow vistas (three views demarked "Marysville Buttes," "Wolf Mt.," and "Sacramento Valley") sliced through it. Prager's original, central vista of the water chain, its pool, and a "glade" extension on the other side of the grass path is the sole surviving perspective, although the woodland growth on the south side of Main Avenue has long obscured Wolf Mountain. A couple of images from a clutch of

surviving archival photos indicate that at one point the tree cover might have been denser. One photo shows seedlings springing up from the lawn. In another, a web of branches intrudes upon what is today an open view up the hill along the water course.

Ultimately, Prager's precise detailing of specimens prevailed over Polk's "forests." In fact, the former "King's Gardener" (the title by which students at the Potsdam school were known) was still engaged with the project as late as the December date on Polk's presentation plan. The Leipzig native had notated the

identity of several trees. Because of these handwritten insertions, some walnuts, the previously mentioned maples, some beeches and birches, and two sentinel magnolias can be securely attributed to the emigrant landscape architect. Although the forest aspect of the plan either was not followed or was radically thinned, today the tree cover—Prager-legacy pines, cedars, an American elm, a chestnut, the magnolias, and more—gives the impression of a wooded area.

By 1906, Polk had directed the installation of the water chain but canted off Prager's vertical line. The

altered orientation focused on the view of distant Wolf Mountain. The architect also introduced an imposing brick retaining wall with iron railing on top that circumscribed the south lawn. It was installed with two matching circular fountains at the corners of the grass terrace. Other Polk proposals, including a giant conservatory and a large swimming pool with a Roman-style pergola outside the clubhouse's indoor

Peonies and iris in the cutting garden.

squash court, were stillborn. Events in San Francisco ensuing from the catastrophic 1906 earthquake shifted attention back to the city. Surviving Empire Cottage drawings, held at UC Berkeley's Environmental Design Archives, indicate that Polk continued to work desultorily on the project up until about 1910. However, by that date Bourn had cast his eyes toward the San Francisco Peninsula. In Woodside, thirty miles south of the city near the Crystal Springs Reservoir, his confidant and constant architect would, between 1915 and 1917, design Filoli, a more sumptuous summer home that would supersede the cottage in the Sierra foothills. (Filoli was one of the first National Trust for Historic Preservation properties on the West Coast. Its ballroom ceiling is gilded in gold from the Empire Mine.)

By 1921, the individual curriculum vitae of the team that created the Empire Cottage had radically diverged. In 1917, Bourn, exasperated by his associate's unreliability, had dismissed Polk from the Woodside job. Polk's rumored drinking and premature death seven years later at age fifty-six suggest there were grounds for the rupture. In a finality of a different order, Prager was deported from the United States on the charge of treason in 1921. (He had made the strategic mistake of returning to California after fighting for his homeland in World War I.) If Bourn was incensed by his architect, he would have, if he had read the small, contemporaneous news items, been truly appalled by the actions of his one-time landscape architect. In stark contrast, in 1920, the San Francisco magnate received France's Legion of Honor Award for his outstanding efforts on behalf of that nation.

In 1929, Bourn sold the Empire Mine and Cottage for good. (Collectively, Bourn and his father bought and sold the property three times.) The usual progression for such a remote spot would be a slow decline and eventual disappearance, but the garden defies that fate. The site's distinction has commanded loyalty: first by the resident Chinese family George and Susie Oyung, originally hired by the Bourns as caretakers, and from 1975 to the present, by the State of California. Where and when the efforts of the California State Parks agency have fallen short, a succession of keen volunteers have lent vital support. Similar to his investments in Northern California's utilities, William Bowers Bourn Jr.'s first venture into landscaping has paid benefits to generations.

Discounting the virulent loyalties surrounding World War I, Bourn's bet on Prager was not misplaced. After the Empire Cottage, he served for six years as the city landscape architect for Oakland. For thirty-five years following his precipitous ejection from the United States, he practiced, until his death in 1960, in Chile, where he is celebrated as the country's founding landscape architect.

# THE LANDSCAPE AT GREEN GABLES

David C. Streatfield

Green Gables in Woodside is one of the most ambitious American gardens produced during the Arts and Crafts movement. A typical garden of this genre was relatively modest in size, reflecting the ideals of fine craftsmanship and regional identity espoused by John Ruskin and William Morris in the later years of the nineteenth century in England. Both the house and garden at Green Gables were designed by Charles Sumner Greene, who, with his younger brother, Henry Mather Greene, realized some of the finest-crafted houses ever built in this country while working together as Greene and Greene. Charles Greene worked

Below: View of the back of the house with its large lawn and pool. The columnar oak on the terrace behind the house replaced an original oak with a spreading canopy, which better framed the house. Opposite: In 1928, Charles Sumner Greene recommended draping the stone walls of the colonnade in Chinese trumpet vine. Today, wisteria grows in its place.

at Green Gables in 1911 and from 1926 to 1928 for Mortimer and Bella Fleishhacker, prominent members of San Francisco's Jewish community.[1]

The Fleishhackers' seventy-five-acre property, with its panoramic views of the Santa Cruz Mountains to the south and west, contained rolling meadows and clumps of coast live oaks. Since the new owners disliked the Japanese-inspired bungalows in Pasadena on which the Greene brothers' reputations were based, their choice of Charles Greene was decidedly odd. They wanted an English house with a thatched roof, like the Devonshire cottages they had seen while traveling. This is what Greene provided on a rather grand scale. The size of the property, the shortage of available water, and the difficulty of adjusting a modestly conceived summerhouse to the dramatic site would make it Greene's most challenging design commission. Over a period of some seventeen years, he created one of his most beautiful and memorable designs.

The garden was designed in two stages. In the first phase, a rectangular lawn was placed below the broadly splayed house and its wide brick-paved terrace surrounding a huge domed oak tree. At the far end of the lawn was a broad, T-shaped pool. This severe design was enlivened only by golden-brown glazed pots placed at the corners of the pool. Beyond the pool, at the top of a steep bank, were plantings of poplars and Atlas cedars (*Cedrus atlantica*) that framed views of the mountains from the terrace and diagonal views across the lawn. The austere design may have been inspired by the simple English landscape garden at Studley Royal in Yorkshire, which Greene had visited in 1909.

Over the years Greene returned to design more projects for the Fleishhackers. The most important was the commission "to do something" with the area lying some sixty feet below the main lawn. This design, featuring a 300-foot-long reflecting pool curved at both ends, resolved the lack of a harmonious link between the garden foreground and the distant mountains. Greene exploited the drama of the site since the water garden cannot be seen from the house. The view from the top of the stairs, over two broad, swirling flights of stairs descending to a wide terrace overlooking

the pool, is one of the most memorable in California. Giant flower pots made of small, carefully graduated brick pieces and their flowers provide color.

A stone arcade at the far end of the pool, partially screening the view, resembles a ruined Roman aqueduct. It is adorned with the same green glazed flower pots that flank the pool. The open arches of the arcade are echoed in arched recesses in the wall below the staircase terrace. These and the bold, swirling forms of the double-branched staircase evoke some of the Italian Baroque gardens in Frascati that Greene had visited on his honeymoon. The planting of two Monterey pines (*Pinus radiata*) at the head of the staircase was another subtle allusion to Italianate design. The artful selection of three different stones for the paving of the staircase and the dark red-brown brick for the balustrade suggested a place of considerable age.

Greene's 1928 planting plan for the colonnade was brightly colored and highly textural with the broad leaves of honey bush (*Melianthus major*) arranged around the columns and coral-colored Chinese trumpet vine (*Tecoma grandiflora*) trained onto the stone. Between the columns, the simple massing of lily of the Nile (*Agapanthus*), with bold orange, red, and yellow cannas behind, created another burst of vivid color. He wrote, "Allow the rear of the border to melt into the taller planting as indicated. By occasionally varying the exact geometric pattern as shown, a natural effect is obtained," adding,

> The seedlings should be set out very close together as the effect needed is one of a complete color carpet and the quality of individual bloom is of no importance. I feel that the beds along the lake must count for as brilliant a color mass as the fields of Wild Flowers, but that they must bloom over the entire season.[2]

Greene's understated references to English and Italian sources were a poetic response to the character of the landscape. Although the clients had dictated the style of the house, the garden was an artistic achievement directed entirely by the designer. It enhanced and emphasized the character of the surrounding landscape by providing views of it and by incorporating materials of that landscape. The exquisite craftsmanship and Greene's appropriation of historicist references resulted in a true celebration of the genius of the place.

Green Gables was passed to the grandchildren of Mortimer and Bella Fleishhacker, who have beautifully maintained the garden. In 2004, they entered a conservation easement with the Garden Conservancy to protect this magnificent garden.

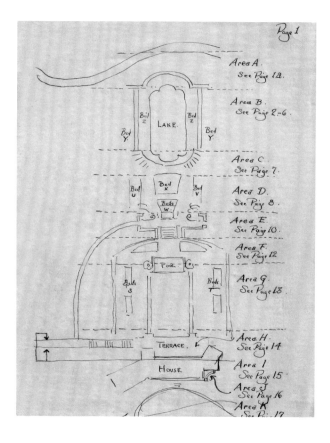

Above: Charles Sumner Greene's 1928 garden plan illustrates the axial organization from the house and terrace to the lower property, where he located the colonnade and "lake" or pool. Overleaf: The allusion to Italianate style in the stone colonnade at the end of the pool blends into the views of the Santa Cruz mountains.

# A RADICAL VISION FOR PALOS VERDES

Christine Edstrom O'Hara

Palos Verdes was the largest new American town designed in the 1920s.[1] The Boston-based Olmsted Brothers landscape architecture firm, city planner Charles H. Cheney, and Pasadena architect Myron Hunt planned the new community on a spectacular coastal site on a peninsula in southern Los Angeles County. The Palos Verdes project was conceived as early as 1914, and it developed during a period of critical regionalism, when its creators sought not only to express American values but also to create a distinctly Californian design. Their aim was to showcase the native California landscape and to demonstrate a new approach to design in architecture and planning, one specific to the history and ecology of California. With an initial design area of sixteen thousand acres, Palos Verdes was the most extensive suburban community commission Olmsted Brothers ever undertook, and it became a long-term project in which the firm continued in an advisory role through 1948. Upon seeing Palos Verdes for the first time, Frederick Law Olmsted Jr. is reported to have remarked:

> How often are men given such an almost untouched great area…the cliffs, the beaches, where the ocean once was, the canyons, the hills and the ocean. May we who are now responsible, place parks, open spaces, roads, not for racing, but to look at the beauty, and may the generations who follow keep this in their minds and plans.[2]

Olmsted Brothers was named after John Charles Olmsted (1852–1920) and Frederick Law Olmsted Jr. (1870–1957), respectively the adopted son and son of renowned landscape architect Frederick Law Olmsted Sr. (1822–1903), who retired from practice in 1896.[3] Along with both brothers, associate James Frederick "Fred" Dawson (1874–1941) managed the firm's Pacific Coast projects. While the firm was prolific, ultimately designing or consulting on more than six thousand projects throughout the United States, Canada, Bermuda, and Cuba, Palos Verdes was not simply a commission but became the personal home of both Olmsted Jr. and Dawson. In a 1922 contract, developer Frank Vanderlip ensured a fluid oversight of Palos Verdes's design and construction phase when he required that "during the continuance of this contract at least one member of the firm of the Olmsted Brothers

Below Left: John Charles Olmsted. Below Center: Frederick Law Olmsted, Jr. taken at Palos Verdes. Below Right: James "Fred" Dawson in Malaga Cove, Palos Verdes. Overleaf: Panoramic ocean view looking north from Palos Verdes to Malibu.

shall at all times be resident at or near Palos Verdes… and Frederick Law Olmsted and James F. Dawson shall both be so resident and available for as much of the time as continuously as they find necessary for the proper direction and prosecution of the work."[4]

Through their residence during the 1920s, Olmsted Jr. and Dawson were able not only to influence the community's taste and control the long-term development of the city, but also to infuse their professional and personal values into the design. In October 1922, the firm opened its first West Coast office in nearby Redondo Beach.

In Palos Verdes, each designer, as well as the developer, had a specific conception and agenda for the community. In response to the site's southern Italian ambience, Vanderlip envisioned an exclusive residential community based on Mediterranean design. Similarly, Olmsted Brothers intended the design to be in accord with the semi-arid Southern California climate. Incorporating ideas of regionalism first tested by the senior Frederick Law Olmsted at Mountain

View Cemetery (1865) in Oakland and at Stanford University (1886), the firm's vision followed its unbuilt proposal for the 1915 Panama-California Exposition in San Diego, a design that endeavored to showcase the native California landscape.[5] City planner Cheney (1884–1943) helped develop Palos Verdes's villages, mixing Mediterranean prototypes with new American planning models.

Attempts to develop a regional California architecture based on the missions—Mission Revival style—began in the late nineteenth century. By the 1920s, the style had evolved into California Mediterranean and Spanish Colonial Revival, borrowing from Europe and Mexico, incorporating Italian, Moorish, Spanish, and

Above Left: La Venta Inn was a restaurant and hotel that acted as the sales office, due to its panoramic views and lush planting. Above Center: Casa del Portal building in Malaga Cove Plaza was constructed in 1929 in California architecture style. Opposite: View of the north entrance to Palos Verdes showcasing drought-tolerant planting, 1925.

Mexican elements. Myron Hunt (1868–1952) called it "Californian," and as chief architect at Palos Verdes, he waged a campaign to officially recognize the California style as the official style for the new community.

As "Directors of Design," the Olmsted Brothers' approach began with a rigorous study of the new region to understand the complexities of the semi-arid and steep site. Fred Dawson began intensive research in January 1914, hiring outside consultants to create detailed topography maps and to conduct hydrology, soils, and temperature studies across the Palos Verdes peninsula. Dawson contacted California native plant expert Theodore Payne regarding the toughness of plants in the region and purchased seeds from Payne's store. Propagation of appropriate plants suitable to the climate was a priority. An on-site nursery was established, and nurseryman Louis Horner was hired to care for and propagate plants full-time.[6] Horner experimented with propagation techniques, including dry farming, and gathered seedlings in the wild as starters for his nursery stock of acclimated plants.

Palos Verdes became the largest unirrigated development in the country at the time through the use of regionally appropriate plants. Realizing that new California residents might not appreciate the dry native and Mediterranean plants, John Charles Olmsted wrote:

> We believe it would be advantageous to do a great deal of landscape planting on lots and residence tracts before they are sold, especially ornamental trees and fruit trees, not only to assist in rapidly bringing large areas into attractive home-like condition, but because so many prospective purchasers know so little about the planting of residence grounds, especially in Southern California where the climatic and soil conditions are unfamiliar to many.[7]

Not only did the firm reduce lawns in its residential design, but commercial areas and parks were lushly planted primarily with native and adapted plants. Park

designs drew from other Mediterranean regions, such as the Moorish prototype for Farnham Martin's Park in the development, with fountains and its copious amounts of local Palos Verdes flagstone. Peripheral low-growing plantings and plants in pots composed the vegetation, and lawns were limited to spaces for recreational needs. The chosen plant palette blurred the design into the nearby borrowed landscape.[8] In fountains, pots, and the unirrigated adjacent native landscape, water usage was dramatically less than was typical in a low-water region.

As a resident of Palos Verdes, Frederick Law Olmsted Jr. came to understand the typical patterns of flood and drought in Southern California and designed in a way to accommodate both conditions. While the planting design required relatively little water, stormwater management for heavy inundations was also a priority. Open space in Palos Verdes was carved out of the profitable hillside and shore-bluff lots, fulfilling multiple functions. Stormwater drainage flowed into open space, minimizing the need for storm drains by diverting water into canyons and other natural drainage channels. Preplanned open space not only preserved the native California landscape but also mitigated the effects of the region's heavy winter rains.

The design of Palos Verdes was completely driven by the existing landscape and climatically compatible forms of urban design and architecture in the Mediterranean region. The flora influenced a regional approach to its architecture, plant selection, and water management, and in integrating buildings and landscape that produced a truly "Californian" environment. While the design expressed new standards and ideals in modern American subdivision planning, at the same time, it created a community that functioned ecologically with the site. Mixed among the "appropriate" aesthetics were new American needs and values: for the automobile, active recreation, and open space within the city. It was a radical approach to design in a new region and an early example of sustainable landscape design on the West Coast.

Overleaf: Moorish design at Farnham Martin's Park with walls faced in local Palos Verdes stone, 2022. Above Right: Fountain, planting, and hardscape design that was emblematic of semi-arid design, c. 1920s. Below: Palos Verdes residents enjoying horseback riding at the north entrance, 1926.

# LOCKWOOD DE FOREST AND THE SANTA BARBARA LANDSCAPE

Susan Chamberlin

The 1924 article "Do Lawns Belong in Southern California?" by Lockwood de Forest Jr. is a landmark in West Coast landscape theory. Or at least it should be, but de Forest's manifesto was quickly forgotten after it appeared in *Garden and Homebuilder* magazine.[1] At the forefront of American landscape architects championing drought-tolerant and native plants, de Forest (1896–1949) is acknowledged as a superb designer of regionally appropriate gardens and buildings that pointed the way to modernism. With his wife, Elizabeth Kellam de Forest, he produced *The Santa Barbara Gardener*, one of the first, if not *the* first, magazines devoted to gardening in coastal California's winter-wet, summer-dry Mediterranean climate.

Written at the beginning of his career, de Forest's seminal article reflects his love affair with California and the Mediterranean region. It lays out many of the principles that would inform his innovative designs: bright green lawns are "foreign and unnatural" against the tawny, summer hillsides of California; spatial considerations as well as views must be considered; "drought-resistant" plants are most suitable; harmony between house, garden, and the natural landscape is essential—for inspiration, look to the classic examples along the southern coast of Spain, Italy, and France. He names useful plants from similar climates, adding that for Southern California gardens the "material that is

The maverick landscape architect Lockwood de Forest in the "Buffalo" car he built.

most natural is, of course, the native shrubs themselves" including *Ceanothus*, California holly or Christmas berry (toyon), wild cherries, wild sumacs, and coffeeberry.[2] De Forest specifies where lawns can be effective, but he cautions, "Don't plant more lawn than you can take care of." He also warns against using lawns against a backdrop of summer-dry hillsides or risk the effect of "an overturned can of green paint."

De Forest would put these principles into practice in the design of his own garden in Santa Barbara's Mission Canyon (1926) and at the Wright Ludington estate known as Val Verde in Montecito; the William Dickinson estate in Hope Ranch (c. 1928); the Santa Barbara Botanic Garden (he began consulting there c. 1927); Arthur Meeker's Constantia in Montecito (c. 1930); and Sterling Morton's Montecito estate (c. 1946). He also contributed to Madame Ganna Walska's Lotusland early in its development. Each is now recognized as a landmark in the history of gardens and landscapes in California thanks to research initially carried out by William Frederick Peters and David C. Streatfield.

De Forest participated in the influential 1937 exhibition *Contemporary Landscape Architecture and Its Sources* at the San Francisco Museum of Art and had

garden commissions in parts of the state ranging from the Bay Area to San Diego. Although he was not a licensed architect, buildings he designed include the house for his family in Mission Canyon; Val Verde's servants' quarters, garages, "Baptistry" garden folly, and art gallery–atrium–pool house complex surrounding the original water tower house designed by Bertram G. Goodhue; the Nicholas Ludington house; the Ernest Watson weekend house; and the Griffith (Tilt) and Reese Taylor beach cottages. The latter's window wall, made from a garage door that opened the living room to the ocean, landed de Forest in *Architectural Forum* ahead of more celebrated avant-garde architects who were featured in the April 1937 issue including Richard J. Neutra, William Wurster, and R.M. Schindler. This method for connecting the indoors with the outdoors is now widespread throughout the United States.

Southern California begins at Point Conception in Santa Barbara County, where the coastline abruptly jogs and the mountains run east–west instead of along the north–south axis typical of most of the state. This means that the city and about half of the county have a south-facing coast, a major reason for the popularity of this area as a resort. Plants with analogs in the

Above Left: For the estate called Constantia, de Forest had a eugenia hedge pruned to the same shape as details on the house façade, utilized various foliage colors, and sited a pool to reflect the mountains. Above Center: El Fureidis, designed by Bertram G. Goodhue and his client, was a firm break from Victorian-era styles. Above Right: De Forest with his horse at the Thacher School in Ojai, where as teenager he began to love the natural California landscape.

CALIFORNIA EDEN

old-world Mediterranean climate are found here and throughout much of coastal California: live oaks, bay laurel, salvia, lupine, and artemisia, with sycamore and willow in the riparian creek beds. There are spectacular spring wildflower displays in the mountain meadows. Bigpod ceanothus (*Ceanothus megacarpus* var. *megacarpus*) dominates the chaparral vegetation blooming white after winter rains. This gives a gray cast to the entire mountain backdrop of the city, which is perhaps the reason de Forest used plants with gray foliage that harmonized so well with the regional hues.

Below: The house de Forest designed for his family in Mission Canyon opens to numerous outdoor rooms filled with drought-tolerant plants. Overleaf: The south lawn axis at the Casa del Herrero is a design by de Forest and Francis T. Underhill.

De Forest was from the generation of designers who created a regional identity for the West Coast following the Victorian era. Constructed throughout the United States in the nineteenth century, Victorian-style houses and informal picturesque-style gardens chock-full of plants took their inspiration from England. In California, enthusiasm for palms and subtropical vegetation was the driving force. Victorian-era health seekers and settlers had been enthralled with palm trees growing year-round outdoors, the fragrance of orange blossoms, and the evergreen olive trees that the Spanish colonists had planted merely for practical reasons. By the late nineteenth century, Santa Barbara was noted for its concentration of outstanding gardens and for its horticulturists and nurseries.

As the Victorian era drew to a close, Santa Barbara became a favored destination for affluent people from the East Coast and Midwest who wanted to escape to a warmer winter climate. De Forest's parents joined them sometime between 1889 and 1902.[3] Around this time, James Waldron Gillespie's El Fureidis in Montecito, east of the city, took its place as a nationally significant example of a new style. Designed by Bertram G. Goodhue and his client as a Persian villa garden and widely published at the turn of the nineteenth century, El Fureidis was axial, architectonic, and more thoughtful in its planting than the gardens of the Victorians. It helped establish Montecito as *the* status place to build in Santa Barbara and was followed by a number of Mediterranean-inspired villas with formal gardens. This style was also favored by the "Hill Barons," men who controlled vast fortunes and vast properties on the hills overlooking the city of Santa Barbara and the ocean.

The natural California landscape is something that the New York–born de Forest had come to love as a teen at the Thacher boarding school in the Ojai Valley, east of Santa Barbara, where he was sent for an education rooted in the outdoors when a Connecticut prep school proved problematic. Matilija poppies (*Romneya coulteri*) grow wild in the canyons of Ojai, where de Forest hiked with his cousin and future client Wright Ludington, also a student at Thacher.

De Forest studied landscape architecture on and off in college. His studies were interrupted when he enlisted in World War I, but he came down with the Spanish flu and never saw action. By 1919, he was in Berkeley at the University of California, where he completed a year of landscape gardening and planting courses and then moved to Santa Barbara to live in his parents' house. He was soon working for landscape architect Ralph T. Stevens, the region's most prominent garden designer. Stevens was the son of the nurseryman R. Kinton Stevens and a former UC Berkeley faculty member. He and de Forest did not get along, perhaps because he thought Stevens had "no imagination."[4] De Forest quit, and before long he was taking a grand tour of Europe with Wright Ludington.

The idea that Santa Barbara should draw upon its Spanish colonial past to create a regional identity began to develop prior to the Panama-California Exposition of 1915 in San Diego, but its influence throughout the Southwest was enormous thanks to Bertram G. Goodhue, the principal architect of the exposition and the style that would become known as Spanish Colonial Revival. Santa Barbara's Community Arts Association, founded in 1920 and led by Bernhard Hoffmann and Pearl Chase, had a vision to unite architecture and landscape architecture with planning and the preservation of historic buildings to create a single, unified cityscape that would evoke a "mythical" Spanish past. "The city itself was to be the designed artifact."[5]

Hoffmann hired architect James Osborne Craig to create the El Paseo open-air shopping complex, which was built and landscaped like a meandering street in Spain around the old Casa de la Guerra adobe. Completed in 1922, El Paseo charmed the public. In 1925, the city was rocked by a massive earthquake that damaged Mission Santa Barbara, destroyed much of the downtown, and broke many of the wedding presents of the newly married Lockwood and Elizabeth Kellam de Forest. Chase's Plans and Planting Committee of the Community Arts Association was ready to assist individuals who needed help, and downtown Santa Barbara was rapidly rebuilt in Spanish Colonial Revival style.

The time was ripe for Lockwood de Forest's career to take off. Wildly creative and completely unorthodox, de Forest and his unconventional wife took Santa Barbara by storm, both socially and professionally. He

De Forest screened out everything that did not contribute to the illusion that his garden stretched all the way to the mountains, although later development in the foothills mars the view today.

was soon engaged by George Steedman to flesh out Francis T. Underhill's revamp of the south lawn axis for the Casa del Herrero in Montecito, which Ralph T. Stevens had completed in association with its architect, George Washington Smith, and Steedman.[6] De Forest did other projects for Steedman later.

The house de Forest designed for his family in Mission Canyon was built around 1926, the same year his first son, Kellam, was born. It is abstract in its reference to Spanish style and was arranged around an open, central atrium and numerous outdoor rooms. Full of innovation and utilizing native, local sandstone, the garden had a lawn of kikuyu grass that was allowed to go brown in the summer to link to the borrowed scenery of the mountain view. De Forest contained this invasive grass with a stone seating wall, then sloped fill soil to the top of a retaining wall along Todos Santos Lane, creating a rock garden and a pond. This elevated the garden to screen out automobiles on the road and everything else that did not contribute to the impression that the garden stretched all the way to the mountains. He lined the driveway with gray olive trees and a hedge of gray pineapple guava (*Feijoa sellowiana*) to link to the mountain color. Relating a garden's colors to the regional landscape "was one of de Forest's most significant contributions to the theory and practice of garden design."[7]

Lockwood de Forest was involved at Santa Barbara Botanic Garden almost from its founding in 1926 as Blaksley Botanic Garden. He provided design advice in various capacities until his death. When he enlisted in World War II, he continued to advise by correspondence. The Santa Barbara Botanic Garden had a powerful impact on botanic garden design because it was the first in California to be devoted solely to native plants and was designed as a park with plants arranged in ecological communities, not as individual specimens. Early sustainable horticulture concepts, such as using native plants to conserve water, began here.

Credit for initiating the Santa Barbara Botanic Garden and its native planting concept goes to Frederic Clements of the Carnegie Institution. Its first designer was Ervanna Bowen Bissell, a botanist and avid gardener married to Elmer Bissell, who would be named the director in 1928. Ervanna shared the role with him when she was named associate director a year later. She laid out most of the garden in its first years and selected plants, often after consulting with de Forest. He also did a number of projects and was a member of the 1937 committee chaired by his father-in-law, Frederick Kellam, that produced the first master plan. A year later, landscape architect Beatrix Farrand (1872–1959) joined the advisory committee at the garden. Her clients were the Bliss family, who had endowed it. Conflict between the older, more traditional Farrand, a founder of the American Society of Landscape Architects, and the maverick de Forest was inevitable. Most writers agree, however, that the compromises each designer was forced to make in deference to the other produced some superior designs. Their meadow is the centerpiece of the garden. Together, de Forest and Farrand designed it as an oval planted with California poppies (*Eschscholzia californica*) and surrounded by native trees that framed a view of the mountains. While they agreed on some things, such as removing parking from the meadow, he disliked Farrand's very formal tendencies, such as her courtyard for the Blaksley Library, designed in association with its architect, Lutah Maria Riggs, in 1942.

Barely into his fifties, de Forest died suddenly of pneumonia in 1949. A front-page article in the *Santa Barbara New-Press* said, "His work had a stamp of originality and artistry that placed him in the forefront of the profession." *Landscape Architecture* magazine's obituary noted that he had "an intelligent feeling for space composition" and handled "his garden arrangements as volumes, rather than as pictures and patterns only."[8] Citing David C. Streatfield's work, Robin Karson concluded, "In their spare, architectonic treatment, emphasis on outdoor living, strong functional and visual relationship of exterior and interior, and ease of maintenance, de Forest's gardens would influence a younger group of West Coast designers, among them Thomas Church and Garrett Eckbo."[9]

Contemporary taste has caught up with Lockwood de Forest. His insistence on good design and harmony with the natural landscape using drought-tolerant and native plants with minimal lawn is usually the approach of landscape architects in California today.

Beatrix Farrand and Lockwood de Forest collaborated on the design for the iconic meadow at the Santa Barbara Botanic Garden, shown in this historic view filled with California poppies.

# BEATRIX FARRAND IN SOUTHERN CALIFORNIA, 1925–1959

Ann Scheid

When Beatrix Jones met her future husband, Max Farrand, she was already a distinguished professional and the only woman among the eleven founders in 1899 of the American Society of Landscape Architects. She moved to Southern California in 1927, when Max became the first director of the Huntington Library in San Marino. Her work in California had begun two years earlier, when she consulted on minor details for Casa Dorinda, the Montecito estate of Anna Dorinda Blaksley Bliss, the mother of Mildred Bliss (Farrand designed Mildred's Dumbarton Oaks estate in Washington, DC). Casa Dorinda was com-

missioned as a winter home in 1916 and designed by architect Carleton Monroe Winslow Sr. with Peter Riedel as its landscape architect. This opulent garden was not, as has been claimed, "landscaped" by Farrand in 1925.[1]

In 1926, Max Farrand, a professor of history and noted scholar at Yale, accepted the "alluring opportunity"[2] to head the newly established Huntington Library in San Marino. Selected by the renowned solar astronomer Dr. George Ellery Hale, Max was clearly an outstanding choice for the director's position. Beatrix's role was less clear.

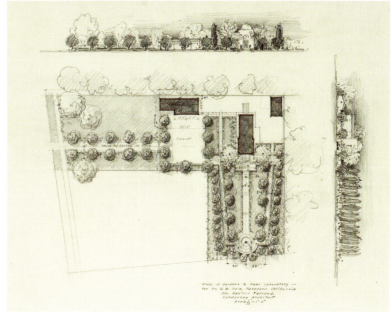

## THE DIRECTOR'S HOUSE AT THE HUNTINGTON, 1930

The Farrands' Huntington home was a guest cottage moved to the north edge of the campus and remodeled by Myron Hunt. Hunt designed a separate studio for Beatrix that was linked by an arbor to the main house, forming an enclosure for the main garden. Behind her studio, Beatrix designed a formal flower garden.

Her layout of the main garden was on a simple axial plan. A terrace along the south side of the house overlooked the lawn, and the vista to the south terminated in a small pool with a wall-mounted fountain centered in a concrete wall at the south end of the garden. On the east, Farrand created an allée of native oaks leading into the rest of the Huntington grounds, giving Max a shady walk to his office in the library. She made use of existing native oaks elsewhere on the property and added mature olive trees, which are easily transplanted and produced handsome gray accents at key points. (The garden has been greatly altered.)

Farrand's reputation as a prominent landscape architect and her position as the wife of the director ought to have given her the opportunity to work on the design of the Huntington estate as it was converted for public use, but it was impossible to displace the longtime head of the gardens, William Hertrich, who had developed the property with Henry Huntington and maintained strict control. Max Farrand noted in a letter before their house was completed, "As conditions are now, even I have to make special arrangements to enter the property any time before 9 o'clock or to remain after 4:30 or to come on a Sunday."[3] Beatrix's inability to bring her talents to bear on the land right outside her front door must have been a source of frustration.

Opposite: The Farrands' house on the Huntington grounds was linked by an arbor to Beatrix's studio. Above: Beatrix Jones Farrand. Below: Beatrix Farrand's study for the Hale Solar Laboratory Garden shows her axial plan centering on the dome of the observatory with elevation views on the sides of the drawing.

## HALE SOLAR LABORATORY GARDEN, 1928

Throughout her time in California, Beatrix Farrand continued designing for clients on the East Coast, spending months working as she traveled back and forth by train. Her first garden in Southern California was for Dr. George Ellery Hale, who had persuaded Huntington to leave his property to the public and who had attracted leading researchers to Pasadena's Throop Institute, transforming it into the California Institute of Technology (Caltech). In 1924, Johnson, Kaufmann, and Coate designed a solar laboratory for Hale's retirement years on the property he shared with

his wife on a lot that was split off from the Huntington acreage near Pasadena. Farrand's early 1928 sketch of the garden shows a formal axial plan centering on the dome of the observatory. An invoice includes consultations with "Miss Bashford," referring to Katherine Bashford, a well-known local landscape architect.[4] Bashford no doubt influenced Farrand's choice of plants for Southern California's Mediterranean climate, which are now iconic in its built environment: Italian cypress and orange trees, native oaks, myrtle hedges (*Myrtus communis*), native sycamore trees (*Platanus racemosa*), strawberry trees (*Arbutus unedo*), and loquat trees (*Eriobotrya japonica*).

along the east–west wing of the main hall opens onto this secluded space. Farrand's plan improved the space and managed the slope of the land by creating an almost square courtyard at grade with the main hall and centered on a fountain located on the west wall of Dabney. A low retaining wall ornamented with graceful, inset concrete benches at either end separated the main courtyard from the smaller upper courtyard at street level. A central north–south walkway executed in flagstones bisected the main space, which was also outlined by flagstone paths. Rectangular panels of lawn and mature olive trees provided a restful color scheme in shades of green and gray, enlivened by Cherokee roses on the courtyard walls. (The courtyard has been altered by the elimination of lawn and other changes to the design.)

Having planned significant portions of the Princeton, Yale, and University of Chicago campuses, Farrand had definite ideas about how the Caltech campus plan could be improved, and she pressed for the adoption of a campus master plan. Mid-1930s memos reveal that she had prepared some preliminary recommendations for the western portion of the campus.[6] No action was taken on her recommendations, perhaps because Caltech had lost almost its entire endowment in the 1929 stock market crash. Farrand's other major contribution to the campus was her plan for a garden south of the Arms Geological Sciences Laboratory. (There is no record of the plan, and the garden was later demolished for new construction.)

By 1938, Farrand had tired of her status at Caltech. She wrote requesting compensation for her work and the authority to have her designs executed. The executive council decided it was not wise "to enter into any formal arrangement" but hoped to seek her counsel in the future.[7] She suggested the campus make future arrangements with another designer, although she agreed to finish the garden around the Arms lab as a tribute to the donors, Henry and Laurabelle Arms Robinson, "as my professional gift to them and the institution."[8] By the time Farrand wrote this letter, she was fully engaged in a much more rewarding project at Occidental College in the Eagle Rock district of Los Angeles, and her long involvement at the Blaksley/Santa Barbara Botanic Garden was underway.

## CALIFORNIA INSTITUTE OF TECHNOLOGY, 1928–1938

Farrand's work at Caltech began shortly after her arrival in Southern California.[5] Her first project (uncompensated) was the courtyard for the new humanities building, Dabney Hall, designed by Goodhue Associates in 1927. Located on the north edge of the campus, it was to be a companion to the adjacent Gates Hall, with which it formed a quadrangle. Farrand used the L-shaped plan of Dabney to create an enclosed courtyard, shielded from the street and the rest of the campus by a wall. A series of French doors

## OCCIDENTAL COLLEGE, 1936–1941

Farrand's most extensive project in Southern California was a major redesign of the campus at Occidental College, undertaken in the last years of the Depression at the instigation of college trustee Charles H. Thorne, who was donating money to build an auditorium. The chosen location for the new building provided an opportunity to rethink the campus layout. Thorne, a Chicagoan who knew of Farrand's work at the University of Chicago, had stipulated that he wanted "Mrs. Max Farrand or someone as experienced" to do the landscape design for the auditorium.[9] Oxy president Dr. Remsen E. Bird offered her the project in 1936, marking the beginning of her five-year-long involvement with the campus, a project that Farrand later wrote "lies very close to my heart."[10]

The original 1913 campus plan by Myron Hunt and Elmer Grey had oriented the buildings along a long driveway running up a steeply sloping hillside. In Thorne's vision, the driveway would be closed, and the new auditorium would terminate one end of an axis lying perpendicular to the slope with the other end terminating at the existing Clapp Library. This plan required constructing four terraces across the slope, enabling the introduction of a traditional campus quadrangle. Other key buildings were already arranged along the long axis of the proposed quadrangle.

Farrand became a key member of the committee implementing a 1935 campus plan by Hunt and his then partner H.C. Chambers. She established a happy, collaborative relationship with the firm and the college. Here Farrand was clearly in her element, having done similar work on other campuses. Alphonzo Bell, a wealthy alumnus, chaired Oxy's Grounds Committee. Bell, Thorne, and Fred F. McLain, the college comptroller, held the purse strings for Thorne Hall, with Bell being the primary source of funds for the landscape. Farrand played a major role in the entire project: she determined the designs and warm tan color for the concrete of the terrace walls and steps and specified that flagged paving be creamy and rough like travertine, that the walks in the central quad section be of decomposed granite, and that asphalt paving for the service roads be colored to match the buff shade of the buildings by rolling-in yellowish gravel. She was insistent that the architects study the level of the new auditorium very carefully in order to successfully "marry" it to the slope and discussed the positioning of steps, walls, and ramps around the building in detail.[11]

Rather than plant small trees in the quad and then wait years for them to grow, she specified mature California live oaks (*Quercus agrifolia*) in boxes. Los Angeles nurseryman R.W. Hamsher boxed trees from

Above Left: Beatrix Farrand was a key member of the team for Thorne Hall on the Occidental College campus. Above Center: By the early twenty-first century, the native coast live oak trees in the Occidental College quad had reached enormous size. Above Right: Although it has been altered, Farrand's Music Building courtyard at Occidental College retains its charm.

the wild, and she chose eighteen of them: four large multi-trunked specimens for the two ends of the quad and four large single-stemmed trees for the center. McLain, who was deeply committed to supporting Farrand's ambitious plans for the campus, broke the news to Bell about substantial budget overruns for the huge oaks, and Bell came through with the funds.

Farrand also designed furniture for the quad: concrete benches and tables, chairs, and teak benches to be arranged along the walks. The teak benches and chairs came from an English firm, Hughes Bolckow Shipbreaking Co., which sold garden furniture made from centuries-old teakwood salvaged from British battleships. Farrand had designed the company's Britannia bench, four of which were shipped to Oxy. Armadale Avenue on the campus takes its name from the source of the benches, wood salvaged from the *Armadale Castle*, a passenger liner converted to World War I service.[12]

Farrand's concerns about Thorne Hall's siting and how it fit into the existing context and the slope of the land led her to suggest creating gentler transitions from the quad to the forecourt and from there to the road behind the building.[13] She proposed a gray-toned planting scheme around the building. In the flagstone-paved forecourt, she placed four fifty-year-old olive trees for shade. Large agaves were obtained from the Huntington and planted on the east side of Thorne with white wisteria atop a wall on the north side. Additional plantings included olive trees on the hillsides and lavender and rosemary close to the building's

walks and entrances, where passersby might brush up against them, releasing a lovely scent.

Farrand went on to design the courtyard of the Music Building using dry-laid brick for the walks. Irises were planted in gravel around the fountain in the court. She specified white oleanders along the front of the building and boxwood to edge the walks in the courtyard (since altered, but still a memorable space).

Recognizing how people create their own paths from building to building, she envisioned "footpaths leading from the buildings [as] short cuts or 'sneaks' through the planting."[14] Farrand's last job at Oxy was a campus plan that included new dormitories. She chose the site for Haines Hall above the quad and used small orange groves enclosed by myrtle hedges to outline the space in the foreground. Her work at Occidental was very satisfying. She proudly wrote to Bell, "Yesterday when Mr. Chambers and I were working on the campus together, he said he thought it one of the loveliest of the small colleges and very largely owing to the beauty of the simple lines in the central quadrangle….With ever so many thanks for the happy work at Occidental which is entirely due to your instigation."[15]

## THE BLAKSLEY/SANTA BARBARA BOTANIC GARDEN, 1938–1950

In 1938, Farrand was appointed to the Garden Advisory Committee at the Blaksley (Santa Barbara) Botanic Garden through the efforts of her client Mildred Bliss, whose late mother, Anna Dorinda Blaksley Bliss, had

endowed the garden in 1926. Farrand receives more credit than she deserves for its innovative design and use of California native plants.[16] This was the concept of Dr. Frederick Clements of the Carnegie Institution. The garden's first designer was Associate Director Ervanna Bowen Bissell, but local landscape architect Lockwood de Forest Jr. worked with Bissell almost from the beginning and helped produce the garden's original master plan.

Now recognized as an important figure in the transition to modernism, de Forest was twenty-five years younger than Farrand and working as the garden's landscape advisor when she arrived. Farrand was older with a preference for traditional, axial layouts. They agreed on many things but also clashed. The meadow they collaborated on adjacent to the Blaksley Boulder is the stunning centerpiece of the garden, but de Forest was never happy with Farrand's formal courtyard for the Blaksley Library nearby. She designed it in association with its architect, Lutah Maria Riggs, who credited her as the consultant on the 1942 blueprint. Farrand retired from the board of trustees in 1950, at age seventy-eight.

## A RETURN TO MAINE

By 1941, Max Farrand had tired of his administrative duties at the Huntington, and his health was not good. The announcement of his retirement in March was met with general dismay. Oxy President Bird wrote to thank the Farrands for many things, including "the making of this campus beautiful beyond compare."[17] Beatrix described the move from California as a "terrible wrench…it is rather a tug at the heartstrings to leave its pleasant surroundings."[18]

The Farrands moved to Beatrix's beloved summer home, Reef Point, in Maine, but returned to California every winter, staying in their cottage at the Valley Club in Montecito. Beatrix continued to winter in Montecito after Max's death in 1945, until just before her own death in 1959. Beatrix left $20,000 to the Santa Barbara Botanic Garden and her books and papers to the University of California at Berkeley.

Above: Haines Hall dormitory at Occidental College with its myrtle hedges (*Myrtus communis*). Opposite: Farrand worked with architect Lutah Maria Riggs to axially align the Santa Barbara Botanic Garden's library courtyard with the Blaksley Boulder, to the left of the path, and the mountain view.

# THE CALIFORNIA LANDSCAPES OF KATHERINE BASHFORD

Steven Keylon

In a relatively short career of twenty-five years, Katherine Bashford would design some of Southern California's most beautiful residences, hotels, churches, and housing projects, often with her longtime partner, landscape architect Fred Barlow Jr. Though she was for the most part self-trained, Bashford, with her confident artistic sense, social connections, and business savvy, was one of the most respected and highly sought-after landscape designers working in Southern California in the 1920s and 1930s. Architects Roland E. Coate, Wallace Neff, Reginald D. Johnson, Gordon B. Kaufmann, and, in particular, H. Roy Kelley repeatedly collaborated with Bashford, trusting her refined style.

Today, Katherine Bashford is primarily known for the splendid gardens she designed during the golden age of grand estates. These gardens used classic historical detail and Mediterranean-influenced hardscape and plant materials while maintaining the regional California spirit. However, Bashford should also be remembered as one of a handful of forward-thinking innovators experimenting with an early transitional modern style. Like her statelier traditional gardens, these creative and contemporary landscapes possessed restraint, dignity, and charm. Still, even greater attention was paid to the indoor-outdoor relationship and its easy, comfortable usability. Her focus on the ecological side of landscape design—emphasizing native California or compatible Mediterranean-climate plant species—makes her work particularly relevant today and worthy of further study.

## EARLY LIFE AND INFLUENCES

Katherine Bashford was born into a respected and influential "American Colonial" family who would become "one of the fine, substantial families of Southern California."[1] Not only were they politically prominent, but they were also socially progressive. Katherine's

"El Molino Viejo," or The Old Mill, was once the mill for Mission San Gabriel. When it was converted into a private residence in the 1920s, Katherine Bashford researched and used plants that had been used during the time the California Missions had been built.

great-uncle, Coles Bashford, was one of the founding members of the Republican Party, a party that was created in opposition to slavery. Later, Coles and his brother Levi (surveyor general and Katherine's grand-father) were part of a group tasked by President Lincoln with organizing the Territory of Arizona. Once there, the brothers opened an upscale general store in Prescott, the Bashford Mercantile Store, which was said to be the largest in the region. Levi's son, Coles Allen, met and married Miss Henrietta Parker in 1879. One of four children, Katherine Emilie Bashford was born in Prescott on August 19, 1885, to Levi and

Henrietta. The family moved to Los Angeles in 1894, where the local newspapers reported on Katherine's many activities, typical of a young high-society girl of the day—teas, debutante balls, beach excursions, and performances. Bashford graduated from the exclusive Marlborough School for Girls in 1905.

After a trip to Europe just prior to World War I, Bashford decided to become a landscape architect.[2] Though never formally trained, Bashford had an instinctive talent for landscape design and a disciplined drive to acquire the proficiency she would need to succeed in this field.[3] It was reported in *California and*

Left: Portrait of Katherine Bashford, c. 1928. Right: One of Katherine Bashford's earliest commissions was done with frequent collaborator Wallace Neff, here for Singer Sewing Machine heir Arthur K. Bourne.

CALIFORNIA EDEN

*Californians* that Bashford "began an intensive course, largely without special instructions, since there was no school in the West at that time, and she desired to study in constant contact with the environment where she was determined to apply her skill."[4] As part of that self-education, Bashford began amassing a large collection of books, folios, photographs, and sketches covering all aspects of landscape design, horticulture, architecture, art, and sculpture.

She opened a small practice out of her home in 1917 and, in 1921, began a two-year apprenticeship with established landscape architect Florence Yoch. Her two years with Yoch exposed her to the workings of the office of a professional landscape architect. Bashford, who was initially drawn to the profession because of her intense love of flowers, gained practical experience with construction and business practices and broader exposure to horticulture. Yoch's influence on Bashford's style would be profound.

In the midst of an unprecedented building boom in Southern California, Bashford made a bold move in 1923 and opened her own large-scale landscape architecture firm in Pasadena. She again traveled to Europe in 1924, where for six months she continued her study of classic European gardens, spending time in Italy, Spain, France, and England. By the end of the 1920s, Bashford's exquisite gardens created in partnership with leading architects and their discriminating clients would be widely published and praised in *The Architectural Digest, California Southland*, and *California Arts & Architecture*.

## THE 1920s —
## THE "GOLDEN AGE" OF GRAND ESTATES

Bashford herself was extremely dignified. Word had it that "Miss Bashford's gardens were dignified and restful," and some say she received commissions because she "behaved like a lady and did not give a hard sell."[5]

An early commission in 1925 turned out to be one of her largest, an enormous estate in San Marino for Edith and Arthur K. Bourne. Bashford worked with their architect Wallace Neff, who designed an expansive Andalusian-style farmhouse on a four-and-a-half-acre parcel. To give the considerable gardens warmth and livability, Bashford's Spanish-inspired landscape design featured intimate, human-scaled patios and outdoor rooms, some containing colorfully tiled benches and fountains, which she made informal with a profusion of potted plants and flowers.[6] Restraint was shown in the planting immediately surrounding the house.

As Bashford explained in an article in *California Southland*, "The architecture of today grows naturally from the soil, springing up with strong, graceful lines that need no blurring base planting to hold them

down."[7] Many of the walled gardens of the Bournes' San Marino estate enclosed spirited displays of boldly flowering color, which lent relief to the expanses of white patio walls and paved walks.

At the Barber residence in Pasadena, designed by architect Roland E. Coate, Bashford's landscape featured a long brick pathway to the front door, bordered on either side by rectangular panels of turf and flanked by rows of fruit trees underplanted with long, exuberant flower beds. Bashford believed these long, flower-lined walks would "make promenades for nervous house dwellers."[8]

At Kencott, the home of Hazel Patricia and Kenyon Reynolds in Pasadena, Bashford overcame a challenging site, which had a bowl-shaped arroyo at the rear of the house, dropping sixty feet below street level. Preserving two massive live oak trees and a small stream, Bashford oversaw the eighty-five thousand hours of labor needed to create terraced rock gardens, ponds, and fountains, built using seven hundred tons of Santa Susana sandstone. Kenyon Reynolds, president of the Pasadena Flower Club and the local Daffodil Club, and the founder of the Pasadena Floral Show, worked with Bashford on the flowering color, which cascaded dramatically down the terraced pathways.[9] In addition to rhododendron and azalea, the flowers included "mats of aubretia, dianthus, sedums, campanulas and other suitable wall plants. Narcissi bring long sweeps of gold, of pure white, of softest yellow, with accents of richer color." One canyon wall was thickly planted in natives, primarily blue varieties of ceanothus—*Ceanothus arboreus, C. thyrsiflorus,* and *C. cyaneus.* Enlivening the flowering color and shades of green foliage were touches of white, such as white birch (*Betula pendula*) and the white-flowering Japanese quince (*Chaenomeles japonica*), its snow-white blooms reflected in a nearby lily pond.[10]

In early 1928, Bashford moved her office from Pasadena to downtown Los Angeles, to the newly opened and prestigious Architect's Building at 816 West Fifth Street. She would remain in this office until she retired. The building was the eye of the creative storm in Southern California and would be the genesis of much of her work for the next fifteen years.[11] The architects with whom Bashford worked most frequently, Reginald D. Johnson and Roland E. Coate, were also on the seventh floor of the Architect's Building in

an adjoining suite of offices. Architect H. Roy Kelley, a good friend and probably Bashford's most frequent collaborator from 1930 onward, was on the eleventh floor.

Bashford found that proximity to the architects fostered an easy means of collaboration in the early design stages, a partnership they all believed would yield superior results.

## BASHFORD AND BARLOW

In 1928, Bashford hired landscape architect Fred Barlow Jr., who had graduated from the University of California in 1926. Barlow didn't look to Europe for design inspiration and was more focused on the garden as a practical means to enhance people's lives. Bashford, naturally drawn to innovation and practicality, responded favorably to his fresh and forward-thinking approach. Theirs would be a mutually respectful and productive relationship.

Though Bashford remained comparatively busy in the first few years of the Depression, by 1933, the strain was showing. Flower supplier Dr. Samuel Stillman Berry, one of her favorite vendors, wrote to Bashford, hoping "that business is not entirely stagnant with you. For my own part, I will welcome even the smallest orders and will give them equally careful attention with the largest."[12] In a letter to Dr. Berry, Bashford echoed his bleak assessment:

I wish I had some immediate requirements for iris or bulbs but things are still very much in the future. Everything is in a strange chaotic state but evolving, I think, into something real for the not too distant future. If I can use some small orders on the little jobs that are going I will ask for prices.[13]

With no work coming in, Barlow took a temporary leave in the spring of 1934 to work for the National Park Service, overseeing teams of young men in Civilian Conservation Corps camps at Yosemite. However, by the beginning of 1936, President Roosevelt's New Deal policies had begun to positively affect the economy and the building industry. In January, Barlow returned to Los Angeles as a partner in the firm known as Bashford & Barlow. These years would be gratifying from 1936 to the beginning of World War II. They would ride an unparalleled wave of creativity and innovation, made even more satisfying as they were honored multiple times by the Southern California Chapter of the American Institute of Architects (AIA). In addition to their countless residential

Above: Landscape architect Fred Barlow Jr. began working with Katherine Bashford in 1928 as her principal designer, becoming full partner in 1936.
Opposite: Katherine Bashford's signature scattered pots of flowering color line an informal pathway at the McDuffie residence.

projects during this period, Bashford and Barlow also did nonresidential work, including the grounds of Pepperdine University, the Chapman Park Hotel, and the Twenty-Fifth Church of Christ, Scientist.

Both Bashford and Barlow had been very active in the American Society of Landscape Architects (ASLA), Barlow joining in 1928 and Bashford in 1930. Bashford was elected a Fellow in 1936, cited for "the outstanding quality and quantity of her work, her high ethical standards as a member of the profession, and her close collaboration with fine architects."[14] Bashford and Barlow were part of a small core group of landscape architects (which included Ralph D. Cornell, Tommy Tomson, Hammond Sadler, and Edward Huntsman-Trout) who, in 1937, broke from the Pacific Coast Chapter of the ASLA to form the Southern California Chapter. Both Bashford and Barlow served terms as officers, with Bashford being elected chapter president in 1938 (she had previously served as secretary to the Pacific Coast Chapter).

Completed in 1937, the spectacular Palm Springs residence of Lt. Col. and Mrs. Howard C. Davidson was an example of *Gesamtkunstwerk*, or total design. The team included the clients, architects Erle Webster and Adrian Wilson, interior designer Honor Easton, landscape architects, and even artist Millard Sheets as the color consultant. Widely covered in the design journals of the day, the house was featured on the covers of *California Arts & Architecture* and *Sunset*, which dubbed the house "The Ship of the Desert" because of its streamlined nautical detail. Responding to the desert climate, with its warm winter and summer evenings, every room of the house opened onto an outdoor patio or deck.

Referencing the shape of the nearby living room, they created a small, semicircular panel of turf, its form emphasized by a bordering arc of grapefruit trees underplanted with gold and yellow flowering annuals, accented with touches of red. Down one level was a small, decomposed granite area for outdoor dining, with Bashford and Barlow's distinctive pots of red-flowering geraniums (*Pelargonium x hortorum*) lining the walk. Barlow described the garden as "a spot for quiet contemplation of the beauties of the desert, a cool and restful place for relaxation and play."[15] All of this was enclosed by a rock retaining wall built with the same granite boulders of the adjacent mountainside. Weathered a deep brown, this retaining wall helped "carry the sweeping architectural lines of the house in the color and material of the site, thus effecting a harmonious tie between the two."[16] The horizontal line of granite continued along the front of the house, where Bashford and Barlow planted a mass of native desert shrubbery.

With the advent of World War II, landscape work came to a halt. In 1943, Katherine Bashford decided to retire with a heart condition slowing her down, leaving Fred Barlow their landscape practice. He died at the relatively young age of fifty, on March 19, 1953. A little more than two months later, Bashford died, at age sixty-seven, on June 3, 1953.

At the Streamline Moderne home of the Davidsons in Palm Springs, Bashford and Barlow created a semi-circular panel of turf, encircled by grapefruit trees and flowering color. A dining patio overlooked the desert below.

# HANNA HOUSE AND ITS LANDSCAPE BY FRANK LLOYD WRIGHT

Julie Cain

Frank Lloyd Wright's design for Hanna House was a deliberate and seamless integration of the indoors and outdoors. He intended that the glass-walled house and surrounding landscape together make use of the four elements—air, earth, fire, and water—to create a multifaceted and continuously changing environment that plays to the senses.

Paul and Jean Hanna, both children of clergymen—as was Wright—were raised in a succession of houses provided by assorted church parishes. This background, combined with a deeply ingrained love

of nature, created within the couple a desire to live their married life in one permanent location in a home of their own design. In 1930, they read Frank Lloyd Wright's Kahn lectures about modern architecture and believed they had discovered a kindred spirit.

They wrote Wright a letter, and to their amazement, the celebrated architect wrote back. A year later, the Hannas visited Taliesin, Wright's home in Spring Green, Wisconsin. Discussion centered around Wright's concept of organic architecture: respect for the site, for the building materials, and for the past, all to be linked with a sensitivity to the client's needs.

Wright approached design with the concept of *Gesamtkunstwerk*—a unity of art conceived from the largest construction to the smallest detail. He achieved

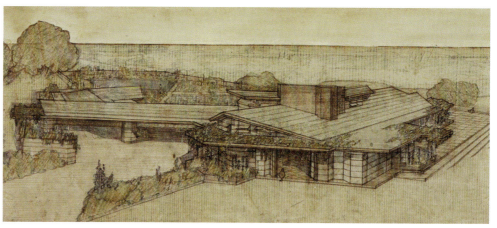

this unity by designing not only the structure but the textiles, fixtures, lighting, furniture, and landscaping.

## THE HANNAS AT STANFORD UNIVERSITY

In 1934, Paul Hanna was invited to teach a summer session at Stanford University. He and his wife, now the parents of three small children, fell in love with California. They found the relatively rural atmosphere of the campus a refreshing change from the crowded urbanity of New York City's Columbia University, where he had been teaching. When Paul was offered a permanent academic position at Stanford's School of Education in 1935, he eagerly accepted.

The Hannas immediately contacted Wright and asked that he begin thinking about a house that would meet their specific needs. On the long cross-country trek from New York to California, they again stopped at Taliesin and spent three days with Wright discussing those requirements. Among other things the couple wanted was a house built into the contour of a hill, with "walls of glass so that we could always be visually conscious of sunrise or sunset, the fogbanks rolling over the hills, or trees and grass in the fields."

When Wright mailed sketches to the Hannas in early April 1936, he noted, "There is so much glass surface that the tracery of wood crossing the glass makes only a delicate screen wall—leaving tremendous visibility." He then mentioned "the unusual shape of the rooms,'" a casual reference to the unprecedented honeycomb design that employed an open 120-degree angle and hexagonals. "You will see, I think, a very direct pattern for simple living in the dining and working arrangement as related to living room and play space and terraces and garden."

The Hannas had requested a house that would cost no more than $15,000 to construct. Their choice to build on a hilly site leased from the university inevitably increased the building expense, causing Wright to raise the estimate to a maximum of $25,000, writing to Paul Hanna, "This a promising young man such as yourself with a job should not find outside the bounds of reason."

Wright routinely underestimated the cost of executing his designs and expected his clients to emulate his own carefree attitude toward money (or the lack thereof). The couple agonized over committing themselves to such a large debt, but ultimately decided to do so. Never dreaming the final price tag would total a staggering $39,000, even after reducing the scope of the original plans, both Hannas maintained that the joy of living with Wright's design far exceeded the heavy financial and emotional tolls involved in making their dream home come to life.

## THE ORIGINAL TREES

Although Wright was considered a building architect, his ability to blend structure and landscape was phenomenal. His creation of Hanna House is a prime example of his innate sensitivity to the environment. He nestled the house into the contours of the hill just as the Hannas had requested, and his design utilized most of the trees already standing on the site. He wrote to the Hannas, "We lose the old tree that is about lost anyway, but the others come in so well that it looks as though we built them with the house."

These trees consisted of native valley oaks (*Quercus lobata*) and a Monterey cypress (*Hesperocyparis*, formerly *Cupressus macrocarpa*). Wright encouraged the Hannas to keep the cypress, even though it stood where the carport was to go. Wright solved this problem by constructing the carport to encompass the large tree.

Above Left: Photo of Frank Lloyd Wright by his client, Paul Hanna. Above Right: Drawing of the Hanna House by Frank Lloyd Wright. Opposite: Most of the valley oaks on the site still remain thanks to the care the Hannas gave them. Overleaf: Paul Hanna's workshop was sited uphill from the house.

A brick container was built around the base of the cypress, and an opening was left in the carport roof through which the trunk could project. Fortunately, the opening allowed for growth; the trunk has greatly increased in girth since 1937, but the tree is now declining. The brick container surrounding the tree suffered storm damage and had to be rebuilt in 1950.

Two oaks originally leaned against the wall of the north terrace; one of these came down during a storm in 1994. Another stood sentinel at the south side of the house, outside the bedroom intended for daughter Emily-Jean. A fourth oak grew along the driveway, and three others resided in the backyard. These trees had a scrubby, unprepossessing appearance when the house was built in 1937. They had never received any pruning, watering, or feeding, and it showed. The Hannas subsequently provided the trees with great care, and the trees responded with tremendous growth over the next four decades. Most of these original oaks are still standing, sharing a symbiotic relationship with the structures Wright designed for the sloping, open hillside.

## A WRIGHT-DESIGNED LANDSCAPE

By means of a series of letters, telegrams, and telephone calls, the Hannas communicated directly with Wright or with his secretary, Eugene Masselink,

throughout the design process. Details of the house and landscape mingle in long lists that moved back and forth between the parties; ideas would be modified according to the cost or the desires of the clients.

Grading and construction of the redwood, brick, and glass house began in January 1937. By April, the plumber received orders to connect faucets for irrigation at the "flower boxes," which were made of concrete faced with brick. Located in various places against all four sides of the house, the outlines of the boxes extended the honeycomb pattern of the house floor out onto the terraces, linking the indoors with the outdoors.

In June, Paul Hanna wrote to the architect, "As soon as possible, we should like to have your landscape layout. We could get the soil in the flower boxes and start our plants. Also, we could plant our shrubs wherever you want them along the retaining walls." Wright responded with a promise that "the landscape layout will be sent along as soon as possible." By this time, the Hannas, like Wright's other clients, had come to realize that time moved much more slowly for Wright

## JUNIPERS, FRUIT TREES, AND FLOWERS

The Hannas took Wright's plant recommendations to heart. A receipt dated November 10, 1937, shows a purchase of eleven junipers from the Charles C. Navlet Company nursery in San Jose. Eight of the plants were of the variety then known as creeping Japanese juniper (*Juniperus chinensis* var. *procumbens*), a smaller version of this feathery shrub with a blue-green color. The remaining three plants were larger, gray-green Pfitzer junipers (*Juniperus chinensis* 'Pfitzeriana').

Between January 1938 and February 1941, the Hannas purchased numerous fruit trees, as well as fruit-producing shrubs and vines. They bought a few plants every month. In their own words:

> We preferred trees, bushes, and vines that earned their keep by producing fruit from our orchard every month of the year. There were over sixty varieties, including several apples, plums, cherries, and peaches. Some trees and bushes were exotic: jujubes, *Myrtus ugni*, ice-cream sapotas, tangelos, and guavas. Other trees produced oranges, lemons, pears, apricots, prunes, loquats, figs, avocados, pomegranates, nectarines, and persimmons. Bushes and vines provided black and red currants, black and red raspberries, boysenberries, loganberries, gooseberries, and four varieties of grapes.

The Hannas purchased a few flowers as well, generally red in color. Two of the flowering plants they bought were an orchid (*Epidendrum* x *obrienianum*) and Gazania 'Fiesta Red.' They also had a fondness for star jasmine (*Trachelospermum jasminoides*).

## OUTSIDE IN AND INSIDE OUT

Wright intended the effects of dappling sun and shade to be felt both outside and inside the house. He made it possible by using large glass walls and clerestory windows that enabled sunlight to reach the interior rooms. Intriguing shadows were created by tree branches and fenestration, as well as the numerous trellises that extended beyond the board-and-batten walls. Breezes flowed easily through the house when the numerous doors were left ajar.

The multiple uses of the outdoors (for the children to play, for dining, for gardening, for relaxing, for communing with nature, and for entertaining) were all paramount desires of the Hannas. The relatively mild climate of the Bay Area provided a perfect environment for their "outdoor living" passion to blossom.

than it did for ordinary mortals. Construction often lagged, while frustrated clients waited impatiently for promised plans to be delivered by mail.

On August 23, Hanna wrote back: "'The planting sheet is just right as a setting for the house. We had a mental picture of flowers in some of the flower boxes. You show only vines and junipers. Could you allow us a few blossoms in these boxes?"

Wright oriented the structure to take advantage of the prevailing natural elements—the terrain, the trees, the views, the wind, and the fall of sunlight and shade were all factored into his design. The numerous terraces that flow around the house anchor it to the ground, and their flat surfaces of hexagonal paving extend the interiors smoothly into the outdoors. The glass walls with multiple doorways that open outward or slide along tracks further unify the indoors and outdoors.

Wright did not specify an extensive plant palette on the landscape plan. He generally preferred to use native plants left in their natural state and would tell clients to transplant natives from the nearby countryside whenever feasible. For Hanna House, he simply recommended non-native, "different kinds of low-lying junipers (to overhang edge)" for the flower boxes. Trumpet vine (*Campsis radicans*) or English ivy (*Hedera helix*) was to be trained to climb each of the five trellises that projected from the carport and house, softening the stark lines of the architecture, as did the native oaks on the property.

The part of the property between the house and driveway was to be left as a natural meadow. Lawn would dominate the back of the property, along with a large flower-and-vegetable garden. Creeping ground cover was to be planted on the hillside that ran along the street below the curving driveway.

Their abiding love of nature was also one of the strongest motivations that drove Wright to create as he did. For him, "nature was the countenance of the divine."

## JAPANESE STONE LANTERNS

The granite Japanese lanterns placed around the grounds at Hanna House are a symbol of the long-running relationship between the Hannas and Wright. The Hannas were influenced by the art objects Wright chose to use in his own homes and gardens; they wished to employ the same in their house and landscape. They ordered several stone lanterns from Japan for themselves, and additional ones as gifts for Wright and the Taliesin Fellows who had helped with the creation of their home. The Hannas later added a bronze seated Buddha and two stone temple dogs from Thailand to their back garden.

## CASCADES, ROCKERY, AND TEAHOUSE

Wright had already designed the cascade in 1937, siting it adjacent to the back terrace. However, construction had been postponed due to the rising cost of building the house. When the Hannas intended to finally build it in 1961, they also wanted to include a rockery and teahouse. Wes Peters, Wright's son-in-law and lead architect of Taliesin West after Wright's death in 1959, refined the cascade details and created a design for a teahouse that blended with the existing house and hobby shop.

When Hanna asked about the "treatment of rocks around cascade and pool," Peters responded to him: "We'll just toss them (à la FLW), and they'll seek a natural position alone." One of the features of the cascade was that it was set to turn itself on at 6:30 in the morning, acting as an aquatic alarm clock for the Hannas.

## THE IMPERIAL HOTEL URN

Paul Hanna became interested in salvaging something from the 1923 Wright-designed Imperial Hotel in Tokyo once it was slated for demolition in 1968. He wrote a letter to lchiro lmmaru, the managing director of the hotel: "We could use anything in stone that was part of the exterior or the interior, or something in glass, or murals or anything else that you think might make an interesting linkage between Frank Lloyd Wright's inheritance from Japan and our own Stanford house architecture."

lmmaru wrote back: "I felt that I must give you this interim report on the stone lantern [*sic*] from our old hotel which we wish to present to Stanford University. It was removed by the wrecking constructor with painstaking care and is in fairly good shape, though somewhat eroded. It weighs over a ton, and they tell me that the removal cost amounted to 300,000 yen." This was about $833 at the time.

The urn arrived in mid-July 1968 and was unpacked in the Hanna driveway amid much fanfare. It had suffered some damage during the voyage, but Paul Hanna was confident it could be repaired. He contacted Wes Peters to help with the restoration, which was successful.

The urn and the house suffered severe damage from the 1989 Loma Prieta earthquake. The house was closed for ten years before it was restored, and the urn sat in a storage crate for the next twenty years. It was restored in 2009 and stands once again within the landscape.

## HANNA HOUSE TODAY

The Hannas did not live to see their beloved home ruined by the earthquake. Jean died in 1987 and Paul in 1988. They had given Hanna House to Stanford University in 1974, after living there for nearly forty years. Moving to a campus apartment due to their declining health, they wrote that what they missed most was "the 120-degree angle flow and complete unity of house and garden."

In 1978, the house was listed on the National Register of Historic Places, and it was elevated to National Historic Landmark status as Hanna-Honeycomb House in 1989. It is closed to the public except for special occasions.

Overleaf: The easy indoor-outdoor relationship is evident on the rear terrace. Left: Due to rising building costs, construction of the pool and cascade with its adjacent steps was delayed until 1961. Opposite: An urn from the Imperial Hotel in Tokyo that Wright designed was relocated by the Hannas to their garden when the hotel was demolished.

# A PLAYWRIGHT'S GARDEN
## EUGENE O'NEILL'S TAO HOUSE

Keith Park and Paul Scolari

Managing the cultivated landscape can be challenging at the Eugene O'Neill National Historic Site in the Northern California town of Danville, which is nestled in the San Ramon Valley, a dozen or so miles east of San Francisco Bay. Perched halfway up a steep mountainside, at seven hundred feet above sea level, the elevated site commands sweeping 180-degree views of Mount Diablo and the San Ramon Valley. The solitude, the landscape, and the climate inspired Eugene O'Neill (1888–1953) and his third wife, Carlotta (1888–1970), to build Tao House, a home-and-garden retreat in a remote spot in eastern Contra Costa County in 1937. In the end, it was those same qualities that drove away the author of such twentieth-century American classics as *Long Day's Journey into Night* and *The Iceman Cometh*.

Just six months after O'Neill won the 1936 Nobel Prize for literature, the couple took $17,500 of the prize money and purchased 158 acres of rural, hillside farmland near Danville. The move west from their home on the coast of Georgia was prompted in part by a desire for privacy and peace so the writer could work without distraction, and by a hope that California's famed climate would invigorate them both. "We have

a beautiful site in the hills of the San Ramon Valley with one of the most beautiful views I've ever seen," wrote O'Neill. "This is the final home and harbor for me. I love California. Moreover, the climate is one I know I can work and keep healthy in."[1]

Opposite: Tao House, looking east towards San Ramon Valley and Mount Diablo foothills in background, with intact walnut orchards on the valley floor. Above: The original 1937 concept for the Tao House, drawn by Frederick Confers. Below Left: Carlotta and Eugene O'Neill inside the walled Tao House courtyard, Danville, California. Below Right: Tao House walled courtyard, looking southeast. Note mature, extant Chinaberry tree in background.

Once on-site, the O'Neills planned and developed the surrounding gardens, orchards, and site amenities with the aid of a landscape architect, landscaper, and gardeners. And before long, the hillside property and its old barn and adobe buildings, which harkened to an earlier, pastoral California, were transformed into the sanctuary they desired.

Much of what is known about their time at Tao House comes from their personal diaries, primarily Carlotta O'Neill's. In her first diary entry regarding the property, on April 22, 1937, she writes, "Gene and I both love the Bryant property....It is more than

we wanted and more expensive." Almost immediately they chose the ideal location on which to construct their new house and garden—the leading edge of the only flat and easily buildable spot along this portion of the Las Trampas Hills range.[2]

Soon after acquiring the property, the couple hired local architect Frederick Reimers to design the house-and-garden complex. For reasons that are unclear, Reimers was soon released from the project, and on May 7, 1937, architect Frederick L. Confer assumed the role.

Access to the site was one of the most immediate issues. A right-of-way was needed. After intense negotiation to secure permission to build a road across a neighboring parcel at the foot of the hill owned by Mabel Kuss, the matter was settled. Mrs. Kuss signed the agreement permitting the construction of a narrow driveway to the Tao House site. "The new road is really a boulevard," wrote Carlotta, "…hope it lasts!"[3]

The O'Neills were actively engaged in the design process and expressed a strong desire for a Spanish Colonial theme, one reminiscent of Casa Genotta, the home they had left behind on Sea Island, Georgia. Confer's original concept for the house and courtyard was significantly different from what was built, at least in scale if not style. The only known design rendering shows a Spanish Colonial/Monterey-style building and a mission-inspired courtyard, containing four equal panels of lawn intersected by stone walkways and anchored by a faux water-well structure as a folly. The final house and courtyard were a scaled-down version of this conceptual sketch.

The name "Tao House" was first referenced by the O'Neills in their respective diaries, soon after moving in on December 30, 1937. It was a rather incongruous name for what was clearly a Mediterranean-inspired building, but at least the courtyard landscape lent some degree of credibility to the name. The O'Neills had the courtyard entry gate painted black and affixed with Chinese characters that translated as "the right way of life." Mai-mai Sze, a Chinese friend of Carlotta's who had been consulted about the Taoist slogan, would later recall, "I didn't think it was particularly apt, but

I thought, what does it matter? if it amuses them. The O'Neills had a naive, romantic idea of China—the wisdom, the pageantry and so forth were superficially conceived and romanticized by them."[4]

Perhaps the most conspicuous landscape manifestation of the O'Neill's interest in Taoism is the zigzag entry walkway leading through the courtyard from the entry gate to the front door of the house. This feature is a reference to the Taoist belief that evil spirits will be confused by nonlinear paths of travel and thus unable to enter a building. While the novelty of this circulation feature likely would have amused arriving guests, from a design perspective, the overall effect was to slow down the rate of travel and compel visitors to experience the landscape around them in a conscious way. For subsequent owners of Tao House, however, this design would prove more of an inconvenience than an amusement.

Of all the designed areas at Tao House, the entry courtyard is the most complex space. It is a rectangle enclosing approximately seven thousand square feet of space, with two large panels of lawn near the entry gate and two narrow strips of lawn nearer the front door. The courtyard contained numerous planter beds, a fishpond, climbing vines, potted plants, a rock garden, and patio space. Interestingly, Confer's conceptual design sketch shows the main entry gate into the courtyard slightly off center from the axis of the interior entry walk and front door. Whether intentional or not, this idiosyncrasy became a significant feature of the final landscape design.

One of the more interesting ornamental trees on the property is the stately Chinaberry tree (*Melia azedarach*), which preexisted the construction of the house. The O'Neills and their architect chose to enclose the Chinaberry tree within the walled courtyard garden and planted turf grass around it—a practical decision that achieved an area of "instant" shade for the patio at the eastern end of the courtyard. Numerous photographs of the Chinaberry tree exist, including one of a series taken for *Life Magazine* in 1943 showing Carlotta and Eugene sitting under the shade of the Chinaberry's canopy. The tree is clearly visible in photos taken during the construction of Tao House in 1937 and was even painted by artist and Oakland resident Marius Schmidt sometime around the turn of the century.

Outside the courtyard there were other garden spaces, though these were less stylized than the

courtyard itself and served more utilitarian purposes. Early in the design phase, Eugene O'Neill expressed interest in having a swimming pool. The pool, constructed downslope from Tao House and adjacent to an oak-studded ravine, was completed and filled in April 1938, and its sloped sides were planted with a ground cover of low-growing silver ponysfoot (*Dichondra argentea*). Access to the pool was by way of narrow brick walkways planted on either side with ground covers of ice plant (*Carpobrotus edulis*) and lippia (*Phyla nodiflora*). Horsetail trees (*Casuarina equisetifolia*) and coast redwoods (*Sequoia sempervirens*) were also planted, providing a sense of enclosure and privacy to the pool area. Based on his diary accounts, the pool was O'Neill's favorite location to relax.

Approaching Tao House from the driveway, visitors were greeted by a circular turnaround in front of the entry gate that was designed around a massive valley oak tree (*Quercus lobata*). The circular bed around the oak was defined by a low hedge of boxwood (*Buxus* sp.) and planted with various ornamentals such as Lady Banks' rose (*Rosa banksiae*), pelargonium*s*, and a fig tree. On the west side of the turnaround drive, the O'Neills planted a semicircular row of plane trees (*Platanus x acerifolia*) to protect the house and courtyard from the strong winds that frequently blew down from Las Trampas Hills. Beyond the plane trees to the west, a small patch of open field marked the transition from the formal landscaped area to a vernacular working space. Opposite this field is an old barn that dates to the time when the property was used as a cattle ranch outpost. The O'Neills did not keep livestock, but they did have numerous chickens in a large coop constructed in 1938 on the other side of the old barn.

As early as May 1938, discussions were underway about expanding the existing walnut orchard at the foot of the steep incline south of the old barn. By 1941, the talk of orchards expanded to include other vacant areas around Tao House, and by February 1941, an almond orchard was established on terraces descending from the east side of Tao House between the entry drive and the pool, and a small kitchen orchard of approximately two-dozen pome and stone fruit trees was established north of the house. The northwest side of the house facing the kitchen orchard contained the servants' quarters, kitchen, and related utility areas.[5]

Providing enough water for all the new ornamental and orchard plantings at Tao House would prove to be daunting, particularly during the summer of 1939, when a bad drought descended on San Ramon Valley. As early as 1937, plans to tap into an existing artesian spring upslope from the property were implemented. A series of three 10,000-gallon redwood water tanks were installed to provide water to the house and grounds through a series of underground pipes. Carlotta recorded several exasperated entries in her diary from 1939, exclaiming, "Our lack of water is ruining our garden…this means our garden must be sacrificed.…Heartbreaking—we have worked so hard!"[6] In the 1990s, two of the three water tanks were reconstructed according to historic preservation standards and are still in operation, providing nearly 100 percent of the landscape irrigation water needed to maintain the gardens and grounds.

During their six years at Tao House, both Carlotta and Eugene enjoyed spending time in their gardens, which provided peace, solitude, and privacy while he was engaged in writing some of his most famous works. Between 1937 and 1943, Carlotta made 475 garden-related entries in her diary, while Eugene recorded just twenty-four. Despite this, the playwright was clearly fond of spending time outside, as Carlotta recorded that among her husband's favorite garden activities were "tacking up" jasmine and fig vines to the house (*Trachelospermum jasminoides* and *Ficus pumila*), pruning "his" privet hedges (*Ligustrum ovalifolium*), and "pruning walnut trees" (*Juglans regia*).[7]

As Eugene's health and ability to write worsened due to tremors in his hands, so did the O'Neills' attitudes to the very isolation they had originally sought in 1937. In a personal letter dated December 4, 1944, Eugene wrote, "One thing our ranch in the San Ramon Valley taught me was that no matter how beautiful the hills and woods and meadows, and a valley of orchards with fertile earth, I can admire it objectively but not in any deep spiritual sense. I don't belong. I am not it, and it is not me."[8] And despite Carlotta's earlier fondness for the country and being away from people, by the end of 1943, she was despondent and wrote to a friend, "I loathe the country, for more than a few days. I always have! I have lied to everyone, & myself, all these years trying to make myself like it!"[9]

In January 1944, the O'Neills sold Tao House to Arthur Carlson and his wife at a substantial loss. Eugene O'Neill's final written word about life in California is found in a letter dated April 27, 1944: "What we do now is that we go east…we have both had enough of the coast."[10]

Upon moving into Tao House in 1945, the Carlsons wasted little time reevaluating the landscape and making substantial changes, particularly within the courtyard. In February 1947, the landscape architecture firm of Osmundson & Staley (known today for their seminal midcentury design of the Kaiser Roof Garden in Oakland) was hired by Mrs. Carlson to redesign the Tao House gardens. The most significant alteration to the O'Neill design was the transformation of the zigzag entry walk into a wider path that led straight from the entry gate to the front door. In other changes to the courtyard, the small fishpond (which had failed as a pond and was filled in as a planter bed by the O'Neills) was bricked over, and the paved patio areas were expanded.

In the late 1940s, *Sunset* magazine profiled the garden makeover in a one-page article titled "'Opening Up' an Older Garden." Three sets of before-and-after photos showcased the alterations and described the work with captions such as, "In garden remodeling, a small change in design will often make a big differ-

ence in livability."[11] Other alterations to the landscape during the Carlson period included construction of a large "new barn" in the 1950s for boarding horses, which functions today as storage and office space.

The large Chinaberry tree that once shaded the patio area was severely damaged in a storm and was removed by the Carlsons for safety reasons. As a result, understory plants that once grew in full shade now suffered under full sun exposure. With rehabilitation

as a preservation philosophy, it has been possible to plant nonhistoric, sun-tolerant plants in this space until a new Chinaberry tree sapling (propagated from the stump of the parent tree and currently eight feet tall) can provide full shade to this corner of the courtyard once again.

Although Tao House and the California climate did little to improve Eugene O'Neill's declining health, they did inspire the playwright's artistic out-

put and ensured his place in the canon of American dramatists. Eugene wrote five plays at Tao House, his last and greatest before leaving the property to return to the East Coast on February 25, 1944. He died in Boston in 1953.

The back porch of the house faces Mount Diablo (not shown) and oak-studded, rolling hills.

# RUTH PATRICIA SHELLHORN, FASLA

Kelly Comras

On July 16, 1955, landscape architect Ruth Patricia Shellhorn pulled out of the parking lot of Disneyland at seven o'clock in the evening. She was heading home from a full-speed-ahead project with Walt Disney and his elite design team to finish a pedestrian plan and landscape design before the theme park opened to the public the next morning. She later shook her head with amusement in describing the professional path that led to her collaboration in creating "the happiest place on earth."[1]

Born in Los Angeles in 1909, Shellhorn was raised by parents who promoted the ideals of hard work and self-determination. They encouraged their daughter at an early age to identify a profession that would make use of her mathematical skills and artistic abilities. Seeking advice from her neighbor, the well-known landscape architect Florence Yoch, Shellhorn determined to become a landscape architect when she was fifteen years old.

In 1927, Shellhorn enrolled in the School of Landscape Architecture at Oregon State Agricultural College (now Oregon State University). An outstanding student, she was the first woman to win the Alpha Zeta Scholarship Cup for highest marks, was awarded the Clara Waldo Prize for Most Outstanding Freshman Woman, and joined the Phi Kappa Phi honor society. In 1930, she transferred to Cornell University for additional training in architecture. She again distinguished herself with honors, served as president of the Psi chapter of Kappa Kappa Gamma, and was named consulting national architect for her sorority.

In 1933, after six years of school, Shellhorn found she was unable to afford her final semester at Cornell. She requested permission to take a double course load before the summer break, but her dean refused; he didn't believe women had the resilience for such an undertaking, and so she left Cornell just four units short of her degree. Seventy-two years later, in 2005, the university determined that she had completed enough units to earn two degrees and belatedly awarded her bachelor's degrees in both architecture and landscape architecture.

Shellhorn returned to Los Angeles during the

Above: Ruth Shellhorn supervising installation of an oak tree in a residential garden, 1939. Right: Ruth Shellhorn and Walt Disney at Disneyland Western Railway station, July 1955.

Great Depression, when job prospects for female landscape architects were bleak. She found occasional work with Florence Yoch and Ralph D. Cornell, both of whom exerted a strong influence on her approach to design. Cornell also urged her to go out and find work on her own. By the late 1940s, Shellhorn had completed several commissions for small residential gardens. Her practice expanded to include wealthy clients with estates in Bel-Air and Pasadena, and she began an association with architect Wallace Neff. Her work also led to commissions from a small group of Hollywood actors: Gene Autry (1950 and 1952), Spencer Tracy (1951 and 1953), and Barbara Stanwyck (1951).

In 1940, Shellhorn married Harry A. Kueser. She later credited her unusually prolific career to the business partnership she and her husband created after he left his banking job to join her office in 1945. He took care of the financial aspects of the business, worked with her in the field surveying smaller properties, and helped supervise job installations, thereby liberating Shellhorn to dedicate herself to the creative aspects of her work. Childless, they were constant companions until his death in 1991.

In 1943, Shellhorn began working on the Shoreline Development Study. A harbinger for restrictions on oil drilling in Santa Monica Bay, Shoreline established a precedent for the goals of the later-enacted California Coastal Act. The project's key recommendations also advocated for the use of public funding for recreation and parkland acquisition, and paved the way for installation of Los Angeles's first sewage treatment plant. In a time and place where a woman's presence was unusual, the study provided her with a satisfying opportunity to work on a project ordinarily reserved for her male contemporaries.

Through professional connections made while working on the Shoreline Development Study, Shellhorn received a recommendation in 1945 to create landscape plans for the Bullock's Pasadena and Bullock's Palm Springs department stores with architect Welton Becket. Other Bullock's commissions with Becket followed, including a 1952 renovation of the much-beloved Bullock's Wilshire specialty store near downtown Los Angeles; a remodel of Bullock's Westwood (1957); Bullock's Fashion Square Sherman Oaks (1962); Bullock's at Lakewood Center (1965); Bullock's Fashion Square Del Amo, in Torrance (1966); and

Bullock's Fashion Square La Habra (1968). Shellhorn completed a landscape design, without Becket, for Bullock's Fashion Square Santa Ana in 1956.

The Bullock's stores and the shopping centers were modernist landscape designs, evoking a sun-soaked, leisurely lifestyle that came to epitomize the Southern California look. Company executives allowed Shellhorn to work directly with site planners and architects from the beginning of each project. She recognized that the shopping experience began the moment a customer pulled into the parking lot, and she designed those areas with a generous number of exuberantly flowering trees and shrubs. On the Fashion Square projects, where different architects designed each of the stores, Shellhorn's goal was to create a harmonious transition between buildings with various architectural styles. She composed beautiful, courtyard-like settings, and redefined shopping as a relaxing and enjoyable activity.

Shellhorn designed other significant commercial landscape projects with Becket including the Western Home Office for Prudential Insurance Company (1947–1957); the Veterans Administration Hospital in Long Beach (1955); the Santa Monica Civic Auditorium (1956); a remodel of Becket's 1950 Buffum's store in Santa Ana (1957); and Mutual Savings and Loan Association in Pasadena (1964). Together, Shellhorn and Becket helped shape a regional aesthetic and elevated the profile of Los Angeles architecture. When

Above Left: The Bullock's Wilshire parking court entrance was designed to reflect the refinement of a gracious home, 1952. Above Center: Bullock's Pasadena was one of the first suburban department stores in Southern California to fully embrace the automobile, 1967. Above Right: The landscape for Prudential Insurance emphasized the indoor-outdoor relationship, 1949. Right: Aerial view of the Town Square entrance to Disneyland, 1955.

the Los Angeles Conservancy celebrated Becket's lifetime achievement in 2003, Shellhorn was the only landscape architect, and only woman, to participate in a panel discussion about his work.

Shellhorn's landscape designs demonstrated sensitivity to scale and context, and she was philosophically committed to creating landscape designs with the ultimate user in mind. These skills quickly became evident in the planning and design phases of Disneyland. Originally hired by Walt Disney just four months before opening day in July 1955, Shellhorn's task was to act as part-time liaison between the Disney studios and landscape architects, Jack and Bill Evans, who were responsible for plantings at the amusement park. But, with separate art directors in charge of each of the five "Lands," and construction of many of the rides and attractions throughout the park already underway, Disney worried that the project might not "hang together." Shellhorn ultimately turned her full-time attention to designing a circulation plan for

CALIFORNIA EDEN

Above: Bold textures of banana palm, schefflera, citrus, and agave, with succulents and blooming ground cover, enliven a corner of the Knapp garden, 1949. Opposite: Lush foliage and brightly-colored blooms enlivened a planter alongside the pool, 1958.

the entire park; creating plans for Town Square, Main Street, and Plaza Hub; and overseeing the design of many planted areas throughout the park. She designed islands of flowers and foliage that mirrored the park's exotic and whimsical themes. She narrowed walkways to create a feeling of suspense at some points, and elsewhere broadened them to evoke a sense of wonder at the stunning vistas. She dramatized the park's centerpiece, Sleeping Beauty Castle, with strategic grading of the surrounding moat, and she tied the many parts of Disneyland together by placing full-grown trees of the same species in different locations throughout the park, successfully evoking the small-town America envisioned by Walt Disney.

Up to the mid-1950s, Shellhorn had worked for male architects, landscape architects, and businessmen. The wives of these men were also some of the Southland's most important figures, and they soon became enthusiastic supporters of Shellhorn's work. In 1955, Dorothy Buffum Chandler, the Buffum's department store heiress and visionary force behind development of the Los Angeles Music Center, would play an especially important role in securing work and recognition for Shellhorn. As an editor at the *Los Angeles Times* (her husband was the newspaper's publisher, Norman Chandler), she nominated Shellhorn for a Woman of the Year award after learning of Shellhorn's work with Bullock's and Disneyland. The ensuing publicity led to a cascade of commissions, many of them initiated by members of a group of wealthy women that included leaders of charitable organizations, benefactors of the arts, writers, actors, and members of the financial community.

In 1956, Shellhorn undertook an original adaptation of a Mediterranean garden for the Chandler home in Hancock Park. The garden was part of a nearly one-acre estate, and Shellhorn worked with Chandler to create a flexible design for entertaining large groups

Above: The Doerr garden featured a formal axis across the main lawn, which was softened by an asymmetrical layout of walking paths and plantings with white blooming flowers, 2012. Opposite: Views from the Avery garden patio looked out over the arroyo, 1986.

of people, as well as more intimate gatherings in a garden setting. To emphasize views from the music room and the dining room into the garden, Shellhorn specified a long, formal panel of lawn, which terminated at a circular fountain backed by an ornamental grille. The transparency of the grille shielded a driveway behind it, but gave a sense of depth and spaciousness to the otherwise enclosed area.

The existing swimming pool was completely renovated, and Shellhorn paid particular attention to the surrounding stonework. After conducting an exhaustive search for a stone color that would work well with the green tones of the pool water, she found a subtle mint-green Arizona conglomerate stone and ordered similarly colored cast stone coping for the fountain, the frame around the grille and the grille wall, three sections of wall in the back garden, and a planter behind the pool.

Shellhorn replaced a badminton court with a densely packed rose garden, painstakingly laid out to distribute colors of pink, apricot, yellow, and white roses in a seemingly random pattern. She also preserved existing trees on the property, including eugenia, orchid tree (*Bauhinia* sp.), flowering crab (*Malus* sp.), crape myrtle (*Lagerstroemia indica*), plum and cherry (*Prunus* sp.), Southern magnolia (*Magnolia grandiflora*), and jacaranda (*Jacaranda acutifolia*).

Soon after, Chandler used her influence as a member of the University of California Regents to secure Shellhorn's selection as the "Supervising and Executive Landscape Architect" for the newly opened University of California, Riverside. Between 1956 and 1964, Shellhorn completed a campus-wide master landscape plan that preserved a major portion of the natural campus arroyos, dry riverbeds lined with trees, which she called "rivers of green." The position also included responsibility for site design and new landscaping, as well as the design of roads, walks, lighting, and utilities on the campus. She subsequently held executive and consulting landscape architect positions for other academic institutions, including Marlborough School for Girls (1968–1993), El Camino College

(1970–1978), and Harvard School (1974–1990).

Shellhorn's residential work in the late 1960s, 1970s, and 1980s represents an exceptionally creative period that showcased her maturing skills, perception, and experience. These included a Hancock Park garden for Nancy and Charles Munger; a Bel-Air garden with native oak trees for Hannah and Edward W. Carter; a sculpture garden for Adelaide and Alexander Hixon, with the architect A. Quincy Jones; a modernization of an English-style garden overlooking the arroyo in Pasadena for Ernestine and R. Stanton Avery; a garden for Ann and Henry T. Mudd for a home in Westwood, designed by architect Roland Coate; and the multiyear rejuvenation of Florence Yoch's Pasadena garden for Harriet and Albert Doerr.

By the time she retired in 1990, Shellhorn had received numerous honors for her designs, including a prestigious nomination as Fellow of the American Society of Landscape Architects in 1971 for excellence in executed work. The award also recognized her service as president of the Southern California Chapter of ASLA. She died in Redondo Beach on November 3, 2006. Her papers and drawings are located at UCLA Library Special Collections.

## PART 2

# PUBLIC PLACES
## WHERE COMMUNITIES GATHER

The public landscape is a place where a community can gather and connect with others and the natural world. The scale of public landscapes varies widely from a park to a streetscape to a nature preserve, yet with the same function: they are places to relax, to recreate, and sometimes to educate the people who visit them.

During the early nineteenth century, parks were not a common component of urban design in the United States, so many people used their only green space, the local cemetery, as a place to experience nature. Visitors were attracted to a new type of cemetery in a naturalistic style derived from the English Picturesque landscape aesthetic of the eighteenth century, which drew its inspiration from landscape painting. Known as the Rural Cemetery Movement, the new style spread from the East Coast at Mount Auburn Cemetery to the West Coast at Cypress Lawn Memorial Park in Colma. Golf courses also look park-like; however, water features, mounded slopes, and tree placement are not strictly for picturesque purposes but are intended to create challenges in the game. Pasatiempo, a golf course in Santa Cruz, has a history that is unusual. It was conceived in the 1920s as a golf course with houses for purchase and other amenities by the woman golf pro Marion Hollins, at a time when women had few opportunities in sports or business. Her golf course architect was the famous Alister MacKenzie, a former doctor.

When laying out streets, planners take into consideration the parkway between sidewalk and road, planting, lighting, and other features that may be limited by civic constraints. Pasadena's marvelously varied, tree-lined streets are the result of a 1907 program to raise property values and create shade. Reflecting California's rich bounty of horticultural options, the numerous tree species provided a sense of place for different neighborhoods in the city.

World fairs, those almost instant cities within cities, require intensive landscape and architectural design. To celebrate the completion of the Panama Canal with its guarantee of quicker access to the West Coast, Californians held two world fairs in 1915: the Panama-Pacific International Exposition in San Francisco and the Panama-California Exposition in San Diego. While both were didactic and drew large numbers of visitors, the two were designed quite differently. The architecture was eclectic at the San Francisco fair, but it was John McLaren, the longtime supervisor of Golden Gate Park, who mesmerized visitors with his inventive plantings that seemed to appear, like magic, out of nowhere.

*"In California's gardens and parks and along its streets there exists today one of the most complete and interesting sets of trees to be found anywhere in the world."*

—Peter Raven in Matt Ritter's *A Californian's Guide to the Trees Among Us*

San Diego's competitive exposition of the same year was intended to be regional in its architecture, landscape architecture, and planning to showcase the young city and boost growth. Its Spanish Colonial Revival buildings and patios inspired people throughout the state to adopt this style for their homes and municipalities. Much of the fair infrastructure remains in Balboa Park. The only remnant of the San Francisco fair is Bernard Maybeck's Palace of Fine Arts in classical Beaux Arts style and its adjacent lagoon landscape.

On the other extreme from cities, preserves such as Anza-Borrego Desert State Park may appear to be completely natural, yet the human touch is found in historic cultural remnants of the Indigenous people, the arrangement of roads and trails, and the selection of scenic viewpoints into the desert badlands. Natural preserves require minimal treatment; however, there are many opportunities for innovation in public landscapes that can provide places of refuge and recreation for people cooped up in a city. One of the most unique was Fulton Mall in Fresno, where landscape architect Garrett Eckbo created an outdoor shopping mall in the 1960s. A forerunner of the trend to focus on people, not cars, a pedestrian plaza replaced a stretch of street. It was enriched by art and references to the local region. Sadly, it was too far ahead of its time; traffic resumed in 2017 when the mall was demolished. However, still extant is the equally innovative Kaiser Roof Garden in Oakland, a park on the roof of the Kaiser headquarters parking lot for the benefit of employees and the public.

Other unique public landscapes described in this chapter include Monument No. 1 in Border Field State Park, erected on the Mexico–California border in 1851. Like many monuments dating back to antiquity, its function was to mark a special place and remind visitors of its historical importance. Strange as it might seem for a police facility, the Los Angeles Police Department (LAPD) rock garden within Elysian Park is representative of a 1920s trend for water cascades in American gardens. It was inspired both by Italian Renaissance master works and Clifton's Brookdale Cafeteria in downtown Los Angeles. The quirky LAPD space is open to the public, as are all the places described in this chapter.

Overleaf: The 1915 Panama-California Exposition in San Diego's Balboa Park touched off widespread enthusiasm throughout California for what became known as Spanish Colonial Revival style. Building in several Spanish-influenced styles were designed by Bertram G. Goodhue and Carlton M. Winslow Sr. with landscape, gardens, and patio plantings by Frank P. Allen Jr. and Paul Thiene.

# BORDER FIELD STATE PARK AND ITS MONUMENT

### Nancy Carol Carter

*"Few places in San Diego have such a defined sense of place. Standing [in Border Field State Park], it's impossible not to picture yourself on a map, standing almost atop the line separating the United States and Mexico, in the southwestern-most corner of the forty-eight states."*
—Rob Davis, photographer, 2010

Eight tons of Italian white marble arrived in San Diego in April 1851. Upon delivery of the unwieldy pieces of stone, buyer's remorse gripped Captain Edmund L.F. Hardcastle, who had placed the order with a Boston supplier one year earlier. However, he had a very specific responsibility to fulfill and took charge of the cargo. He arranged military barges to float the four heavy pieces to the south end of San Diego Bay, where they were loaded onto gun carriages for transport to a precise point on a bluff overlooking the Pacific Ocean.

Hardcastle, a US topographic engineer, assembled the marble pieces to create a solid foundation topped with an obelisk. On July 14, 1851, only one year after California became a state, he dedicated this fourteen-

foot-tall edifice as Monument No. 1, a marker of the initial point of the boundary between the US and Mexico, as established in 1849.

Having lost the war with the United States, Mexico relinquished more than half its territory to its northern neighbor in the Treaty of Guadalupe Hidalgo. A joint boundary commission surveyed the new 1,952-mile border. Mexico hoped to retain the useful natural harbor at San Diego and a generous land bridge between the Baja Peninsula and the Mexican mainland, but the boundary was drawn south of the bay and south of the Tijuana River estuary.

Along with the ruins of Mission San Diego de Al-calá, Monument No. 1, standing on what came to be known as Monument Mesa, was a popular Southern California tourist destination during the nineteenth century. The monument attracted more than one hundred thousand visitors annually when railway service was established. Military uses of the land adjacent to the monument grew in the twentieth century, reducing access and stemming the tide of tourists.

Opposite: John Russel Barlett's 1852 drawing of the "Monument at the Initial Point on the Pacific." Below: Pristine growth of native plants at Border Field State Park in 2022.

## FEDERAL OPERATIONS AND THE CREATION OF BORDER FIELD STATE PARK

The US military presence at the border was increased when Mexico erupted into revolution in 1910. After General Francisco "Pancho" Villa conducted a cross-border raid in 1916, the US Army established a camp in San Diego County, near Monument No. 1. The army expanded its uses of the camp, named "Border Field," but it was the navy, after World War I, that began buying up the entire southwest corner of the United States. The navy added an additional 245 acres in 1941 and constructed several buildings and bunkers. In the 1950s, with the outbreak of the Korean War, Border Field became home base for all helicopter squadrons of the Pacific Fleet.

For almost fifty years, Monument No. 1 and its historical significance were lost to the public, although in 1951, the San Diego Historical Society received special permission to hold a ceremony marking the one-hundredth anniversary of the placement of the initial boundary marker. Ten years later, the navy deactivated Border Field as an operational base. California voters approved funds in 1964 to acquire Border Field as a state park. Meanwhile, real estate speculators who had bought up nearby farmland were pushing a different agenda and mounting an intense federal

lobbying effort. The development scheme called for encapsulating the Tijuana River into a concrete flood control channel. Once the flood-prone river was constrained, an upmarket marina would be planned, along with commercial and housing development. Opponents of the concrete channel sought to preserve the ecologically important Tijuana River estuary and discourage development in this unique space.

The fate of the federal land was determined in 1971, when President Richard Nixon announced that Border Field would become part of his "Legacy of Parks" program, in which surplus federal land was transferred to states for recreational uses; 372 acres were transferred to the State of California as Border Field State Park. While granted scant attention initially, these park lands were home to invaluable historical, archaeological, and botanical resources. It is believed that the California missions founder Junípero Serra and the accompanying Spanish military contingent led by Gaspar de Portolá entered Alta California in 1769 by following the ancient trails of the Indigenous peoples crossing the new state park. By turning the land into a state park, a potential treasure of Indigenous artifacts, and the more recently constructed bunkers of World War II, were preserved. Likewise, Border Field State Park protected the best habitat of succulent plants on the Southern California coast and a nearly

Plants such as chollo cactus (*Cylindropuntia* spp.) thrive at Border Field State Park. Opposite: Birds in Tijuana River Estuary, an estuary and wetland at the mouth of the Tijuana River.

pristine growth of other native vegetation. In fact, it was the only US habitat for some plants, and it was the location in which the type specimen for certain species had been discovered years earlier.

First Lady Patricia Nixon traveled to San Diego in August 1971 to dedicate the park and deliver a message of binational unity and friendship. She greeted surfers who had been assembled to demonstrate the recreational potential of the new park. Then the small, barbed-wire border fence separating the United States and Mexico was cut so that Mrs. Nixon could greet the crowd of Mexican citizens who had gathered to see her. "I hate to see a fence anywhere," she said, while signing autographs and admiring babies on the Mexican side of the border. "I hope there won't be a fence here too long….We're good friends."[1]

Mrs. Nixon's comments articulated a vision for Border Field State Park that would place it among the exclusive society of international cross-boundary parks. Exemplars dated back to the 1920s and 1930s, with parks celebrating peace and friendship on the Canadian border. Mexico took the lead by building

a beautifully landscaped park with a wide set of stairs leading up to Monument No. 1 from its side of the border. However, the former navy training fields on the US side remained undeveloped.

## FRIENDSHIP CIRCLE AND OTHER PARK DEVELOPMENTS

Park improvements were slowed by uncertainties over the exact park boundaries, and continuing advocacy for a concrete flood control channel on the Tijuana River. A report from the US Corps of Engineers disappointed real estate developers by making a strong case for preserving the natural course of the river and its richly populated estuary. This home to 170 bird species was called "the finest saltwater marsh remaining along the California coastline" in 1972.[2] Only a portion of the estuary was protected within Border Field State Park, but efforts to preserve the entire estuary gained support and eventually succeeded. Today the Tijuana River National Estuarine Research Reserve is known as a biodiversity hot spot and operates under a state-federal partnership. It is recognized by the United Nations as a "wetland of international importance."[3]

Despite delays in building roads and additional amenities within the new park, visitorship soared to more than ten thousand per month within the first year. Eventually a picnic and barbeque area intended for use by people from both sides of the border was created at Friendship Circle, a landscaped park enhancement incorporating Monument No. 1 and celebrating the harmonious relationship between people of the US and Mexico.

Border Field was a popular meeting place for families living on different sides of the border, but the practice of casual boundary crossings was receiving more scrutiny. The idea of creating a cross-border international park celebrating peace and friendship faded as news reports increasingly described the park as a magnet for undocumented immigration and the passing of contraband. An enhanced Border Patrol presence and a sturdier barrier meant that people had to communicate through the mesh of a border fence. Still, friends and relatives gathered to visit from their respective sides of the border. Others enjoyed the panoramic views and the hiking and horseback riding trails at the park, although swimming and beach use declined due to water quality problems caused by the repeated discharge of untreated sewage into the Tijuana River on the Mexican side of the border.

## OPERATION GATEKEEPER AND THE US DEPARTMENT OF HOMELAND SECURITY

Political pressure on the federal government for stricter border control led to Operation Gatekeeper in 1994, a policy aimed at halting illegal entry into the United States. This controversial strategy targeted the San Diego portion of the border and exerted intense pressures on Border Field State Park. Among other changes, Monument No. 1 was flanked by a tall and inhospitable metal fence.

The border changes wrought by Operation Gatekeeper pale in comparison to those imposed by the Department of Homeland Security, the agency created after the terrorist attacks of September 11, 2001. In San Diego, scientists, the California Coastal Commission, environmentalists, preservationists, and park officials were rendered powerless in their efforts to protect the Tijuana River estuary, the cultural and natural habitat of Border Field State Park, and access to public lands and Monument No. 1. Some of the more objectionable proposals of Operation Gatekeeper for additional fencing and construction across Border Field State

Far Left: Pat Nixon greeting attendees at the dedication ceremony, 1971. Left: Tijuana River Estuary, an estuary and wetland at the mouth of the Tijuana River, 2011. Below: Border Field Monument divided by the Mexico-California border.

Park could no longer be forestalled. Lawsuits based on endangered species and environmental protection legislation were dismissed because the head of Homeland Security was authorized by statute and presidential decree to waive all environmental and other laws impeding border fence construction.

Homeland Security seized ownership of 150 feet of land running immediately along the boundary and began heavy construction in 2008. To create the flat road and fence bed desired by border agents, 2.1 million cubic yards of dirt were needed to fill Smuggler's Gulch, a half-mile-long canyon. To locate this immense amount of landfill, construction crews looked no further than the mesas of Border Field State Park and scraped them, despite documentation of the botanical importance of these natural areas. In addition to altering the cultural landscape of Border Field State Park, construction work devastated the unique native habitat of each mesa. This construction poses a continuing threat to the ecosystem of the estuary because denuded hillsides and the new earthen berm supporting the road produce sedimentary runoff.

## THE MONUMENT AND BORDER FATES

Captain Hardcastle's Monument No. 1 has suffered many indignities in its long history. One of the worst is losing its first-place standing. When the border was subjected to a new survey, the count of boundary markers began in El Paso, Texas. Through the process, the historic *first* boundary marker on the United States–Mexico border became the *last*. The initial border marker was ingloriously renumbered as Monument 258 and is known today by that designation.

The monument fell from its place as a top tourist attraction in the nineteenth century, to become an unnoticed and forgotten relic for almost a half century.

When the monument once again opened to public view, the pressures of undocumented immigration ended its brief life as the centerpiece of a park intended to celebrate international peace and friendship.

Worse prospects for Monument No 1 exist. It is inaccessibly trapped in a no-man's-land between unsightly double border fences. Moreover, the land upon which it stands no longer belongs to Border Field State Park. The Homeland Security agency is said to be contemplating a cession of this strip of land back to Mexico, an action that would redraw a portion of our national boundaries and transfer ownership of Captain Hardcastle's carefully sited monument (a nationally registered historic place) to another country.

All is not lost at Border Field State Park, but it must be recognized that the potential for public enjoyment of this park's beautiful setting and native landscape was not fully realized before these attributes were severely—and perhaps permanently—compromised. Efforts to rehabilitate the native habitat, improve visitor facilities, and save the remaining cultural elements of the park are ongoing, but success is far from assured. Perhaps never to return is the idealistic vision of an international peace park on this section of the United States–Mexico border. Harsh geopolitical realities now make such a plan appear sadly fanciful and quaint.

# THE LEGACY OF PASADENA'S TREES

Ann Scheid

Pasadena, founded in 1874 near Los Angeles, is famous for its Tournament of Roses Parade and Rose Bowl football games, but it is also notable for its elegant rows of mature street trees. Planting trees in rows to border fields or public spaces was customary in ancient Greek and Roman times, continuing in the Middle ages to delineate paths in hunting parks. In Amsterdam in the 1600s, the city required trees to be regularly spaced along canals. Allées of trees in double rows became regular features of royal gardens, urban promenades, and eventually city streets.

When architect Arthur Heineman proposed to the Pasadena City Council in 1907 that the city begin planting street trees, he started a program that has made Pasadena one of the outstanding tree cities of California. Heineman argued that street trees would improve individual property values, make the city more attractive to tourists, and provide much-needed shade from the strong Southern California sun. Heineman estimated that six thousand trees planted along city streets would be worth one hundred thousand dollars in added property values in five years.

Opposite: Spring blooming jacaranda trees form a purple-flowering tunnel. Below: An allée of plane trees (*Platanus x acerifolia*) line a country road in Provence, southern France about 1920.

Orange Grove Ave., Pasadena. Cal.

Pasadena's initiation of a street tree plan was in line with progressive city governments of that era throughout the United States. By the beginning of the twentieth century, street trees were considered standard urban amenities, along with water and sewer systems, street lighting, pavement, curbs, and gutters, as well as public parks, schools, and libraries. In Pasadena, the city government planted the trees in the parkways, the narrow strip of public land between the sidewalk and the street. While trees had long been planted along roads and streets, this had usually been at the initiative of private property owners and not the responsibility of the municipality.

Pasadena's earliest settlers recognized the beauty of the landscape: a mesa dotted with native coast live oaks (*Quercus agrifolia*) at the foot of forested mountains and bordered by verdant canyons and arroyos, where willows (*Salix laevigata* and *S. lasiolepis*) and California sycamores (*Platanus racemosa*) grew. Pasadena's original plan from 1873 laid out the streets to preserve existing oaks. These venerable old trees, standing in the middle of streets or at prominent intersections, survived into the early years of the automobile, with the last one being removed in 1916.

Pasadena was already an important tourist destination by the early 1900s, and its civic beautification plan was in the spirit of the City Beautiful movement. Acting on Heineman's suggestion, the city of Pasadena established a tree nursery. A Tree Commission, formed in 1908, designated tree species for specific streets. By 1916, some seventeen thousand street trees had been planted, and there were thirty thousand trees in the city's tree nursery. By the 1920s, Pasadena was planting five thousand trees annually and, with over four hundred miles of tree-planted parkways, Pasadena

Above: In the early days of Pasadena, enormous, native coast live oak trees were preserved in the middle of many streets. Opposite: Acid green camphor trees, native to Asia, in Pasadena's Prospect Historic District. Overleaf: Native coast live oak trees line a street in Pasadena's Bungalow Heaven Historic District.

could rightfully claim to have more trees per acre and per capita than any other city in California.

Unlike eastern and midwestern cities, where the American elm was the tree of choice, Pasadena took advantage of its benign climate, where almost anything would grow, given sufficient water, and chose exotic species from around the globe as well as native species to populate its streets. This has resulted in a varied "urban forest." Pasadena has usually followed a tradition of planting a specific tree species on each street, which creates distinctive urban spaces—sometimes a corridor, sometimes a tunnel of green—contributing to the aesthetic quality of each street and giving them a special character and identity. A unified look is thus achieved even though the architecture of the buildings may be quite varied.

In the early years, California peppers, native Monterey cypress, and eucalyptus were popular probably due to their fast growth and drought tolerance. California peppers (*Schinus molle*, actually native to Peru) were planted along the main street, Orange Grove Avenue (later called Boulevard). Monterey cypresses (*Hesperocyparis*, formerly *Cupressus macrocarpa*) lined part of Colorado Street, the principal cross street and later the main commercial street of the city, renamed Colorado Boulevard. Photographs from the 1880s show trees along other major streets, including Fair Oaks Avenue. Photos from the early 1900s show California pepper trees along Colorado Boulevard east of the city center.

The earliest notable collection of trees was located at the most prominent intersection of the settlement. Jeanne Carr, horticulturist and friend of John Muir, planted a forest of trees on her forty-two acres and named her place Carmelita (little grove). She had befriended Muir when he was a student at the University of Wisconsin, where her husband, Ezra, was a professor. The relationship was so close that Muir referred to Mrs. Carr as his "spiritual mother." Carmelita boasted over ninety species of trees from all parts of the world, including native trees, some planted from seeds brought by Muir from his wanderings in the California wilderness. Mrs. Carr planted Monterey cypresses along the road bounding her property. They formed a low hedge where Cherokee roses and grapes were allowed to scramble, producing a somewhat wild effect while providing spring bloom and fall color. Carmelita survived as a public park on a dozen acres until the mid-twentieth century, serving as an unofficial arboretum in the growing city. The property, planned since the 1920s as the site for an art museum, was redeveloped in the 1960s when the museum (now the Norton Simon Museum) was built. Most of the landmark trees

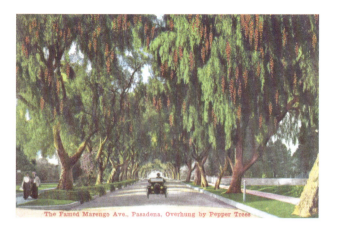

The Famed Marengo Ave., Pasadena, Overhung by Pepper Trees

Above: Morengo Avenue, with the feathery foliage and red berries on California pepper trees, was a tourist favorite. Opposite: Lemon-scented gums mark the entrance to the Athenaeum faculty club at Caltech.

were felled to make way for the museum's parking lot and for a freeway extension.

The fate of Pasadena's trees has usually not been taken lightly; newspaper articles document emotional pleas to protect and preserve them. In the early 1900s, residents decried the mutilation of trees that were in the way of electric wires. When Colonel Wentworth proposed building his massive Hotel Wentworth (later the Huntington Hotel) among the ancient coast live oaks of the Oak Knoll area in 1906, he had to promise to save as many trees as possible. When the city developed Tournament Park as the site of the annual Rose Parade festivities, again the loss of native oaks was protested. Affection for native oaks was so great in the 1920s that they became the principal street tree in the city. Parks superintendent Gilbert Skutt declared that he wanted Pasadena to become an "oak city." His legacy is documented in the Street Tree Plan of 1940: of Pasadena's 392 streets, 136 of them were planted in coast live oaks. Although most of the native oaks in the Pasadena area are this species, other native oaks such as the evergreen Engelmann oak (*Quercus engelmannii*) and deciduous valley oak (*Q. lobata*) are also widely planted. In the 1940s, horticulturist Mira Cullin Saunders wrote a letter to the editor of the *Pasadena Star News*: "In the recent noticeable tendency to use oak trees so widely we are unquestionably creating a problem for future citizens, because as the oak approaches maturity it becomes too massive and too broadly spreading to make a suitable tree for parkings [parkways]."

Six species of oaks made up the preponderance of street trees in 1940; among the ninety-three designated species planted on Pasadena's streets, there were nine kinds of acacia, ten kinds of eucalyptus, and seven kinds of palm. Today there are more than 200 species found along Pasadena's streets, although not all

conform to the Master Street Tree Plan. While residents have planted many notable and exotic trees that later became significant landmarks, the overwhelming number of Pasadena's trees are city trees on streets and in parks. In the beginning, residents selected the species to be planted on their street. As the city grew and new tracts were developed, this became impractical, and the Parks Department began to designate tree species for specific streets. Following the early selection of the California pepper tree for Pasadena's main boulevard, it was planted along other streets as well, the most famous being Marengo Avenue. Hand-colored postcards of this street with its tunnel of pepper trees became a tourist favorite, showing the overhang-

ing feathery branches with large patches of red (artistic license!) to indicate the red berries.

Oaks still form impressive tree tunnels along many streets, including on South Arroyo Boulevard and on Mar Vista, Michigan, Chester, and Holliston Avenues in the Bungalow Heaven Historic District. Palms are another favorite street tree. Planted a century ago, impressive stands of Mexican fan palms, also known as skydusters (*Washingtonia robusta*), line North Mentor Avenue and also Earlham Street. Orange Grove Boulevard, where the Rose Parade begins, is lined with the native California fan palm (*W. filifera*) alternating with mature southern magnolias (*Magnolia grandiflora*). Native to Asia and India, mature camphor trees form green tunnels on Prospect Boulevard and San Pasqual Street (*Camphora officinarum*, formerly *Cinnamomum camphora*). A small street, Rutan Way, is still lined with an impressive stand of incense cedars, which are native to Oregon and Northern California (*Libocedrus decurrens*). Jacaranda trees form a purple-flowering tunnel in the spring on South El Molino Avenue and along East Del Mar Boulevard. Arden Road displays fine specimens of native California sycamores, which can lean and branch out easily on this street of open lawns.

Evergreen eucalyptus trees, native to Australia, have played a major role in the history of street tree and ornamental planting in Pasadena and throughout

many coastal regions of the state. The largest species are little-used now, but their image remains in paintings, photographs, and advertisements from the first half of the twentieth century when their graceful silhouettes symbolized the California landscape to tourists and California residents alike. Eucalyptus seeds arrived from Australia in the 1850s and were spread by the nursery trade. Even native plant enthusiast Theodore Payne promoted the eucalyptus as a regionally appropriate plant. There are hundreds of species. Exceptionally fast-growing blue gums (*Eucalyptus globulus*) were popular for windbreaks and can still be found in agricultural areas.

While the huge blue gum eucalyptus is a problematic species, as ornamental trees in the landscape, many eucalyptus species have had an enormous influence throughout California. In Pasadena they remain as street trees in a few places. There is a notable stand of lemon-scented gums (*Corymbia*, formerly *Eucalyptus citriodora*), planted by the legendary landscape architect Florence Yoch, lining the entrance driveway to the Athenaeum faculty club at Caltech.

Pasadena's older parks still contain fine specimens of early tree planting. Central Park and Memorial Park, both established in 1906 in the center of town, display some trees from that early period. Historical photos of Memorial Park show a row of California fan palms bordering the west side of the park along Raymond Avenue. Now mature, the palms function as street trees and bear witness to the history of the city. In Central Park, which was re-landscaped by Theodore Payne and Ralph Cornell in the 1920s, several large deodar cedars (*Cedrus deodara*) date at least from that period, if not before. Singer Park, given to the city by the Singer family in the early twentieth century, boasts a large deodar cedar, a massive eucalyptus, and a rare example of the clumping European fan palm (*Chamaerops humilis*), the only palm native to Europe. Washington Park, created in an arroyo in 1921, has four memorial oaks planted in honor of important figures in the conservation movement: John Muir, John Burroughs, Theodore Parker Lukens, and Dr. Garrett Newkirk.

As in the early years, controversies about trees continue in Pasadena. The main street, now Colorado Boulevard, has been through numerous tree designations. California pepper trees were replaced in the 1920s by queen palms (*Syagrus romanzoffiana*).[1] This choice may have been made to provide an appropriately tropical setting for the annual Rose Parade, Pasadena's advertisement to the world of its mild winter climate. That designation changed in the 1970s to the Indian laurel (*Ficus microcarpa*), which provided lovely shade but was the bane of shopkeepers, who complained about heaved sidewalks, broken sewer lines, and most importantly, obscured advertising signs. By the 1980s, when the Old Pasadena Historic District began to experience commercial success, the businesses demanded a change, resulting in the current planting of ginkgoes (*Ginkgo biloba*) alternating with queen palms (again!) along the section of Colorado Boulevard traversed by the Rose Parade.

However, this plan was not instituted immediately, leading to the infamous "Midnight Massacre," when the city cut down a half dozen stately *Ficus* trees in the middle of the night, two days before a scheduled demonstration to save them. Reverberations traveled to the city council, which decreed that no healthy public trees are to be removed in Pasadena. Unfortunately, some of the ginkgoes turned out to be females, causing the business owners to complain once again, this time about the noxious stench of the fruit. In compliance with the "no healthy tree removal" policy, city staff have experimented with various washes and injections to reduce female fertility. With new females revealing themselves every season, this may be a "fruitless" effort.

Mindful of Pasadena's historic legacy, the city has charged a subcommittee of the design commission with reviewing all changes to the Master Street Tree Plan and all requests for removal of public trees. The Urban Forestry Advisory Committee (UFAC) contends with everyone from discontented property owners, who just don't like the tree in front of their house, to neighborhoods who want their street tree variety changed, to developers who want to remove trees blocking their projects, and numerous other complaints. The committee also has the difficult task of determining tree species to be planted when a large project, such as new sound walls along the 210 freeway, requires the removal and replanting of trees.

Street tree planting is no longer proceeding at the pace of five thousand plantings a year as in the 1920s; now the number is closer to one thousand a year. Many streets have gaps where trees need to be replanted. Many more have nonconforming trees added by property owners who have no knowledge of the Master Street Tree Plan and its intent to create uniform street corridors. Administrative changes in the city bureaucracy have also weakened the street tree planting program. Still, we can be thankful that there is enough attention paid to trees in Pasadena to warrant a committee to watch over them.

Climate change and drought conditions have forced the city to emphasize water-saving measures, resulting in property owners cutting off irrigation to the trees in their parkways. Members of UFAC have a difficult task in educating the public about the responsibility of property owners to water street trees. Without that, Pasadena's trees, many in serious decline, may not survive in sufficient numbers to provide the shade, cooling, and aesthetic values that Pasadenans have come to expect.

# CYPRESS LAWN AND THE RURAL CEMETERY MOVEMENT

Russell A. Beatty

Not far from San Francisco, Cypress Lawn Memorial Park in Colma is the terminus of a westward migration that began in Boston, where a new type of cemetery—the "rural cemetery"—was conceived in the 1830s. At the time, a landscape aesthetic was evolving in New England based on the eighteenth-century English Picturesque landscape garden. Nature was no longer perceived as a frightening wilderness to be avoided, and the integration of art and nature became a common theme. The heritage of the English landscape garden, with its groves of trees, winding paths, meadows, and lakes evoking a rural scene, was the inspiration for Mount Auburn Cemetery near Boston.

## MOUNT AUBURN CEMETERY

By 1825, Boston had expanded from a village to a major city. With new industries and waves of immigrants, it became so densely occupied that there was no longer space for burial grounds. Public health became a concern. Citizens believed that poisonous gasses emanated from graves and that burial grounds would contaminate the city's wells. Cemeteries were typically barren and treeless. The Romantic-era rejection of the horrors of death, the embrace of melancholia and sentimentalism, and a newfound interest in horticulture and landscape aesthetics served as catalysts for improving cemeteries.

Above: Mount Auburn Cemetery near Boston in Picturesque style inspired the Rural Cemetery Movement. Opposite, Above: Lone Mountain Cemetery, later renamed Laurel Hill, was considered an impediment to expanding the city of San Francisco. Opposite, Below: Businessman Hamden Holmes Noble developed Cypress Lawn Cemetery.

Dr. Jacob Bigelow proposed the idea of a rural cemetery to be developed outside Boston. This coincided with the Massachusetts Horticultural Society's need for an experimental garden to grow and display the latest plants. Across the river near Cambridge, a wooded parcel was purchased and renamed Mount Auburn. Thus, in 1831, with the efforts of Bigelow, society president Henry A.S. Dearborn, and Alexander Wadsworth, the project to combine a cemetery with a horticultural garden was launched.

Mount Auburn Cemetery was laid out as a Picturesque landscape where curvilinear roads and paths were carefully planned to control views, and new plantings of trees and shrubs were added to enhance the natural scenery. It served as a metaphorical garden for the dead as well as the living. The design of Mount Auburn inspired numerous other cemeteries, and it became a popular park.

## THE RURAL CEMETERY MOVES WEST

As the rural cemetery style moved westward, it left behind the landscape in which it evolved and for which it was well suited—a landscape of forest, glade, and meadow in a moist, temperate climate. Describing the rural cemetery's westward migration in "The Park Cemetery," Gunther Paul Barth wrote, "Each leap in its westward migration moved the park [rural] cemetery further from the soil and climate that favored its existence, its creation, its maintenance." Despite the fact that natural conditions changed to a drier, less hospitable climate, the cultural framework reached the West Coast intact. As with many other aspects of the developing West Coast culture, the frontier was modeled on "tasteful" East Coast counterparts, which, in turn, were patterned after England and Europe. In California, the Rural Cemetery Act of 1859 was based on the eastern precedent of pastoral cemeteries, such as Mount Auburn, as an alternative to bleak burial grounds with their regimented tombstones.

After the heady years of the gold rush in California and the completion of the transcontinental railroad in 1869, San Francisco emerged as a city from a boomtown of gimcrack housing and nomadic fortune seekers. With a population of nearly 150,000 by 1870, a cemetery that once seemed far outside the city limits became engulfed in residential development and was soon the target of land speculators. Dedicated as Lone Mountain Cemetery in 1854 and renamed Laurel Hill Cemetery, the large cemetery property was viewed as an impediment to municipal progress as the city began to expand around Lone Mountain. Vandalism and a lack of maintenance led residents of the new neighborhoods to complain. Newspaper writers fanned the flames of anti-cemetery sentiment, including the familiar claim that invisible, poisonous gasses from the dead threatened public health.

Hamden Holmes Noble (1844–1929) helped shape San Francisco into a civilized city following the rough-and-tumble years of the gold rush. A successful businessman, member of the Stock Exchange, mining entrepreneur, and pioneer developer of hydroelectric power in Northern California, he was still energetic at age forty-eight and looking for new endeavors. In his autobiography, he described driving with a friend past Laurel Hill Cemetery in 1892 and noticing its dilapidated condition. His friend said, "Noble, there is big money in starting a cemetery, at the same time doing a great thing for San Francisco." That afternoon Noble went to Laurel Hill. After concluding that there was a margin for profit in a cemetery, he began searching for suitable land and decided that a large site in San

Mateo County was an "ideal location." Noble secured a bond on the property and formed the Cypress Lawn Improvement Company with one hundred thousand shares of one dollar each, then used the money he raised to buy the land and build an office, a chapel, and a granite gateway in Mission Revival style. Although Noble had some knowledge of arboriculture and loved nature, he admitted he knew nothing about the cemetery business, so he traveled east, visiting Mount Auburn and several cemeteries inspired by it.

## DESIGNING CYPRESS LAWN

Noble borrowed the character and design of eastern rural cemeteries for the development of Cypress Lawn. He believed that his cemetery should be nonsectarian and open to all faiths and ethnicities. There is no

Overleaf: Cypress Lawn Memorial Park in Colma was a tourist attraction. Above: This Norman-style gate marks the entry on Hillside Boulevard. Opposite: Curvilinear roads at Cypress Lawn may have been inspired by the books of Andrew Jackson Downing, while evergreen trees, such as these yews and Monterey cypresses, have symbolized eternal life from time immemorial. Lawn and trees were intended to soothe mourners with natural beauty.

record of who actually prepared the original plan for Cypress Lawn, nor is there any record of who laid out the planting scheme. Most authors attribute the design to Noble, but there are no documents to verify his role because all his records were evidently lost in the 1906 earthquake and subsequent fire that destroyed much of San Francisco, including the office of the Cypress Lawn Improvement Company.

With no formal training in landscape design, civil engineering, or architecture, Noble probably did not prepare the initial survey and master plan for Cypress Lawn. His close involvement, however, is clear from his autobiography. A confident, self-made man, Noble likely immersed himself in the task of learning to plan and design cemeteries just as he did in pursuit of his other business endeavors. His comprehensive tour of eastern cemeteries is evidence for this theory. He probably consulted one of the most influential English writers on garden design and horticulture of his time, John Claudius Loudon, the author of *On the Laying Out, Planting, and Managing of Cemeteries: And on the Improvement of Churchyards*, published in 1843. Loudon was the mentor of Andrew Jackson Downing, whose 1841

CALIFORNIA EDEN

*A Treatise on the Theory and Practice of Landscape Gardening, Adapted to North America* was an essential reference for anyone promoting the art of "rural improvement."

There is no doubt that Noble had a clear vision of what Cypress Lawn was to become and how it might be laid out. He hired a superintendent who had worked at a cemetery in Detroit, Michigan. Noble's autobiography indicates he collaborated closely with this superintendent in the initial development of Cypress Lawn, but that he did not understand the climatic conditions of the West Coast:

> I well remember one day I had told the gardener to plant some pine trees in section "D" for a windbreak and to plant some palms nearby. He said: "Mr. Noble, that will never do, as conifers and palms never grow in the same locality." I answered that there were lots of things done in California that couldn't be done elsewhere and that I intended to do lots of things at Cypress Lawn that had never been done anywhere.

Whatever his sources or inspiration, Noble achieved remarkable success in a very short time. The September 1892 issue of *The Resources of California* included a glowing description of Cypress Lawn in an article promoting San Mateo County. It noted that the entry gateway was under construction and that more than four thousand cypress and eucalyptus trees bordered the main avenue with beds of flowers in bloom—all in just five months after the cemetery was begun.

Noble was active in the cemetery's management and introduced reforms for funeral services to reduce the gruesome aspects of burials. He oversaw the excavation of the lake, the design and construction of the West Entry granite gate, and planting.

Noble had considerable expert help. A Scotsman, Alexander Davidson, was his superintendent at Cypress Lawn from around 1900 until he died in 1917. According to his granddaughter, Alberta Foster, Davidson had previously worked for John McLaren, the superintendent of Golden Gate Park. Davidson is said to have been responsible in part for the layout of trees in the cemetery.

## THE HISTORIC EAST SIDE

The cemetery's initial acres were laid out in 1892 on the east side of El Camino Real (expanded later and called the East Campus). The massive Mission Revival–style entry gate framing Cypress Avenue gave Cypress Lawn a distinctive Western regional expression that departed from the design of gates with an Egyptian motif, so popular at rural cemeteries on the East Coast. This granite stone archway, created by B. McDougall & Sons and completed in 1893, reflects the new Mission Revival architectural style. The Victorian era, based on Eastern and English sources, had run its course. Architects and theorists who sought a style appropriate for the West looked to the roots of California's Spanish colonial mission period and to Spain and the Mediterranean region for models because their climates were similar to California's. In addition to the entry gate, the 1893 Columbarium, with its tiled, dome-shaped roof, was also in Mission Revival style. However, the Victorian preference for exotic palms and lawn remained strong.

The Norman-style towers that flank the other entrance on Hillside Boulevard were a departure from the Mission Revival theme. Evidently, Noble conceived of the idea for his Norman towers from the very-similar Washington Tower at Mount Auburn, but in a bit of one-upmanship, he built two towers instead of one. This created another ceremonial gate.

Many later buildings at Cypress Lawn reflect the classical style of architecture derived from ancient Greek and Roman sources, and the main chapel is Gothic Revival style.

The layout and design of the landscape at Cypress Lawn consistently adhered to what a Cypress Lawn brochure of 1898 called the "lawn plan." This was an open greensward planted with trees, meant to soothe mourners by surrounding them with beauty. The brochure stated that fences, copings, and "artificial irregularities" around the burial plots were prohibited to permit "Nature" to "develop her perfection and blend with true art." It was also a way to let the statues and

Eucalyptus Hardwood Nursery, Monterey County, California

Overleaf: The 1893 Mission Revival-style granite gateway for Cypress Lawn was a Western regional expression distinguishing it from Mount Auburn Cemetery near Boston. Above: Nurseries propagated thousands of fast-growing eucalyptus trees in the nineteenth century. Right: Ranging in color from scarlet to orange, red-flowering gum trees attracted visitors to Cypress Lawn. Also not native, palm-like dracaena and Canary Island date palm were meant to evoke the exotic California landscape.

monuments stand out free from clutter and enhance the picturesque atmosphere. The private monuments were works of art, designed by such prominent local architects as A.C. Schweinfurth, Arthur Brown Jr., T. Paterson Ross, J. Francis Ward, and Herbert A. Schmidt. A system of "Perpetual Care" relieved burial lot owners of landscape maintenance and ensured that Cypress Lawn never looked neglected.

## LAYOUT OF ROADS, LAKES, AND PONDS

Not surprisingly, the sophisticated layout of roads, sections, and burial plots in the historic east side reflects the principles of design of early rural cemeteries. Cypress Avenue serves as a spine to which visitors would always return from its looping side roads. The alignment of roads is curvilinear and gently flowing uphill through groves of trees, which lends mystery and surprise around the bends and through views framed by vegetation. Each of thirteen sections is divided into numerous burial lots of varying sizes laid out in grids. Despite the rigidity of these grids, the layout appears informal at ground level because it is diffused with trees and shrubs. Breaking from this layout, Section D (the Iona Churchyard) contains a road in the distinctive form of a Celtic cross, the result of an agreement for the exclusive use of these plots by Episcopalians.

A shallow water table proved beneficial for Cypress Lawn and its pumping facility. It afforded the opportunity to dig artesian wells for irrigation and to fill a lake, which was created near the entry drive off El Camino Real. The lake is now fed by a series of smaller ponds that were constructed around 1920. A grotto-like structure serves as the source of water from an artesian well. These features created a beautiful parklike foreground for the east side of the cemetery and attracted migratory and local birds.

## PLANTINGS

Most of the trees that were favored during the early period of Cypress Lawn were conifers (recommended by Loudon for their air of solemnity) and broadleaf evergreens. Many of these trees are still found growing in the historic east side. Even though the early brochures referred to the landscape setting of Cypress Lawn as "a background of Nature's trees and flowering shrubbery," all the plantings were actually installed from nursery stock on what was originally a treeless, agricultural site and initially kept alive with artificial irrigation. From photographs and an inventory of existing old trees, the "Nature" at Cypress Lawn is revealed. The dominant trees seen in old photos are palm, eucalyptus, and cypress.

Native to Australia, eucalyptus species are well adapted to coastal California's climate and soils. Annual growth rates of ten feet or more for blue gums (*Eucalyptus globulus*) made them well suited for establishing quick cover. During the late nineteenth century, untold acres of blue gum eucalyptus had been planted in California by entrepreneurs who hoped to make fast money from a quick-growing supply of hardwood. Though blue gums proved impractical for timber, they remained popular for windbreaks, parks, and roadside plantings. Native Monterey cypress (*Hesperocyparis*, formerly *Cupressus macrocarpa*) was employed in similar capacities. Nurseries carried large stocks of these trees at low prices and would have been able to supply the thousands of trees that were planted at Cypress Lawn during the 1890s. One species of eucalyptus was a favorite—the red-flowering gum (now classified as *Corymbia ficifolia*). With its brilliant scarlet-to-orange blossoms in summer, it was specifically mentioned in ads to attract visitors to Cypress Lawn via the streetcar.

The palm was another highly attractive tree to Californians who emigrated from the East Coast seeking a mild climate and tropical-looking landscape. The Canary Island date palm (*Phoenix canariensis*) had long been used in the Mediterranean region to provide a dramatic effect at entries and lining driveways. At Cypress Lawn, the entry drive from El Camino Real

to the main gate was lined in this elegant fashion. A circa 1895 photo shows the driveway lined with stout Canary Island palms interplanted with tall Mexican fan palms (*Washingtonia robusta*).

These trees and a few long-lived shrubs at Cypress Lawn tell a story about cultural influences and preferences in horticulture and landscape design. Plants go in and out of fashion, as does any other cultural artifact. Certain plants are signatures of various periods. The Victorian era is expressed in bold, exotic species collected and planted for their individual beauty, form, or color. Easterners who came to coastal California delighted in the great array of plants imported from around the world during the mid-nineteenth century, which could be grown outdoors. Many of these tropical and subtropical plants were seen only in conservatories back east. People who had visited Spain and the Mediterranean region discovered the similarity of those landscapes and climates to California's. In the early twentieth century, tired of the garishness of Victorian landscapes, architects and landscape architects designed buildings and gardens to emulate Mediterranean models—though few could relinquish their affection for lawn.

At Cypress Lawn, these cultural preferences are evident in the plantings within the historic east side. They reflect the taste for the exotic and the desire for fast growth, common in California during the late nineteenth and early twentieth centuries. Some species are indicative of the nursery industry's heavy emphasis on drought-tolerant, evergreen trees imported from Australia and New Zealand—such as *Eucalyptus*, *Pittosporum*, *Metrosideros*, *Grevillea*, and *Araucaria*. It is not unexpected that we would find the evergreen trees that have been traditionally associated with death planted in cemeteries because of their symbolism of eternal life: English holly, yew, and Italian cypress, and for mourning, deciduous weeping willow. A few other deciduous species that are tolerant of wind, as well as Mediterranean species and conifers such as Lawson cypress, deodar cedar, blue Atlas cedar, and plume cryptomeria, can be found mixed with the trees above.

Another tree widely used for windbreaks and evident in early twentieth-century photographs was the native Monterey pine (*Pinus radiata*). Also seen in old photos of Cypress Lawn are two other surviving trees of dramatic appearance that were popular among Californians of the period. Dracaena (*Cordyline australis*) is a palm-like plant native to New Zealand. Its stiff, spiky leaves lend an exotic air to the landscape. The Norfolk Island pine or star pine (*Araucaria heterophylla*) is a conifer but not a pine. Native to an island near Australia, Victorian-era Californians liked this odd-looking tree

The Flood Memorial mausoleum was moved from Laurel Hill Cemetery (formerly called Lone Mountain) to the West Campus at Cypress Lawn.

because of its rigid symmetry of tiered branches and conical form. Though most shrubs have a shorter life span than trees, a few old broadleaf evergreens remain, and others are readily identifiable in historic photos, especially around the lake. As seen in a circa 1930 brochure, topiary work once spelled out "Cypress Lawn Memorial Park" on the slope above the lake.

## CYPRESS LAWN TODAY

There are no records or plans documenting the progress of the developing landscape at Cypress Lawn during the early years, but photos and promotional literature confirm very rapid growth. By 1898, the cemetery brochure proudly boasted that "[we] now have a cemetery complete in every respect." Most of the blue gum eucalyptus trees that grew in the historic east side are gone for a variety of reasons. Today, no one knows why or exactly when the palms that lined the main entry drive were removed.

Cypress Lawn has grown, with more property in Picturesque, "lawn plan" style (and additional chapels, mausoleums, and monuments). Of particular note are the one hundred acres on the west side of El Camino Real that were added as the twentieth century began.

Called the West Campus, it features the Laurel Hill Mound, where the remains of approximately thirty-five thousand early San Francisco residents were moved from Laurel Hill Cemetery (formerly called Lone Mountain Cemetery) around 1940 when it was forced to close. Most of these "Pioneers" were reinterred at Cypress Lawn in unmarked graves. Because relatives were willing to pay to relocate it to Cypress Lawn, the Flood Memorial is an exception.

Cypress Lawn Memorial Park is a unique example of the eastern rural cemetery movement on the West Coast that has remained little changed. Despite the less-hospitable climatic conditions where it was established, it can serve as a model for continuing the legacy of the Picturesque landscape as long as water for irrigation is available. That the plantings have survived and grown so well is a testament to Noble's vision and the knowledge of those responsible for the planting. The rehabilitation of the historic East Campus landscape included renewed maintenance and the replanting of many of the old tree species in the tradition of the rural cemetery. This ensures that it will continue to be "complete in every respect."[1]

# JOHN McLAREN
## LANDSCAPE MAGICIAN OF SAN FRANCISCO'S 1915 EXPOSITION

Laura A. Ackley

Fairgoers at the 1915 Panama–Pacific International Exposition in San Francisco enjoyed the mechanical and handmade marvels inside the exhibit palaces. But outside, they were enchanted by the spells a horticultural wizard cast in the gardens and courtyards. Immense beds of flowers in full bloom magically changed overnight. Trees nearly seventy feet tall stood where the San Francisco Bay had lapped months earlier, and a twenty-foot-high wall of living green, touched with delicate lavender blossoms, served as the world's fair's boundary for several blocks.

*Sunset* magazine said that John McLaren, chief of landscape for this great world's fair, needed to use the "technical training of an engineer, a gardener, and a botanist" to realize his astounding and revolutionary plans for the landscape design of the celebration.[1]

From its earliest stages, McLaren partnered with the other designers of the 1915 fair, also nicknamed

Left: View west down the Avenue of Palms at the 1915 Panama-Pacific International Exposition. Above: John McLaren at Golden Gate State Park, 1927.

"the Jewel City." He believed "the relation between a beautiful structure and its grounds…is a very definite one. At the great Exposition the landscaping became as much a part of the general plan as were the architecture, the color, the sculpture, and the lighting." In addition to developing subtle landscapes to match the "moods" of the great central courts of the fair, he implemented several wholly new, spectacular landscape techniques that astonished viewers.[2]

On the gala opening day, February 20, 1915, the fair's flower beds flourished with golden color in homage to the Golden State. The fifteen-acre "South Gardens," designed in the formal French manner, greeted crowds streaming through the main entrance with a tapestry of several hundred thousand gilded blooms. A mass of bright, upright daffodils covered the beds. Yet a few weeks later, when the daffodils were losing their luster, they mysteriously disappeared one night to be suddenly supplanted the next morning by a profusion of yellow tulips. And when the tulips were spoiled by rains, a cloak of bright pansies took their place overnight.

Fair guests were puzzled by his ability to maintain the flower beds in constant bloom while changing their varieties with such rapidity. McLaren had conspired with Jules Guérin, chief of color, to plan a rotation of plantings in keeping with the colors of the exposition buildings and the turning of the seasons. In the South Gardens alone, the plantings transitioned from the gold of opening day to brilliant red, then to palest pink as the nine months of the fair passed. Many of the necessary hundreds of thousands of seedlings were cultivated in Golden Gate Park, where McLaren had been superintendent since 1887. Working on the foundation created by engineer William Hammond Hall, he transformed great swaths of the park from inhospitable dunes into a verdant playground for San Franciscans, with bridges, lakes, waterfalls, trees, and fern-lined dells.

McLaren's secret was a system of planting that relied on his thorough knowledge of each plant's blooming habits. In the South Gardens, his large team of gardeners had planted the daffodils, tulips, and pansies simultaneously before the exposition opened. The daffodils bloomed first, and as they wilted, the chief sent his corps out at night to clip them off and pitch them onto trucks for removal, leaving the tulips, which had been sprouting beneath the daffodils, to burst forth seemingly instantaneously. Similar overnight removal of the tulips revealed the golden carpet of pansies growing lower still. Each rotation required about 250,000 plants, and *The American Florist* estimated that approximately two million flowers were used in the South Gardens over the run of the fair. The canny McLaren used the same quick-change technique not only through the cycles of the South Gardens but also in several of the opulent courts.[3]

Another bit of the Scottish-born McLaren's wizardry was more subtle—the placement about the grounds of hundreds of fully grown trees, some more than sixty-five feet tall and weighing as much as sixteen tons apiece. Many of these ornamented the central portion of the exposition, which was built on the location of a former seventy-one-acre saltwater lagoon that had not been filled in until late 1912.

Where recently tides had inundated the site to a depth as much as twenty feet, now lofty trees thrived. Many patrons simply did not believe they had not been planted there decades earlier. "Visitors who could not believe that the great palms and eucalyptus trees surrounding the exposition palaces were transplanted had to be told gently and firmly that the bay had covered the whole central portion of the site when construction began; especially where some of the largest trees stood. Some believed, but many lacked faith," wrote the exposition's official historian, Frank Morton Todd.[4]

McLaren had recognized that early proposals to bank thirty-foot-tall trees against the sixty-five-foot-high walls of the palaces would cause the trees to look small and "out of proportion to their magnificent backgrounds." So, he started a nursery of tree seedlings in Golden Gate Park in April 1912, later moving the plants to Tennessee Hollow on the Presidio grounds.

The audacious Scot also sent a cadre of "competent men" out in early 1912 to canvas the surrounding counties for impressive specimen plants, the owners of which were then asked to donate the trees. If they consented, which the proud landholders often did, a new version of "side-boxing" was implemented. A huge "knife," seven feet long, was driven through the roots on all four sides of the tree. Three inches of soil were inserted between the cut side roots and the box sides that were driven down around the tree, and then the plant was carefully tended, allowing new systems of small side roots to develop before the tree was removed. Six months or more later, the box bottom was added, and the trees were shipped to the site.

In November 1912, the eucalyptus and acacia seedlings for the Jewel City stood only twelve to

eighteen inches high. Two years later, consistent with their exceptional growth rates, the eucalyptus trees had attained heights of twenty-five to thirty feet and the acacias, fifteen to twenty feet. Starting in the summer of 1913, some of the largest trees were the first to be planted at the fair. This allowed them to attain their full growth, some topping the high ivory walls by the time the exposition was in full operation. Thus, said McLaren, the trees lent "an effect of permanency and long-established growth." Many of these sturdy varieties were planted along the north walls of the fair, where they were able to withstand the bay winds without interfering with the marvelous vistas across the silver-blue waters. The eucalyptus trees were joined by pointed cypress, some of which were donated by San Jose's Oak Hill cemetery.[5]

Parallel to the sheltered, southerly wall of the exposition's palaces, McLaren created a splendid pedestrian esplanade, the "Avenue of Palms." This broad path was lined with 350 stately trees, most of which had been shipped to the site from the California Nursery Company in Niles, located about twenty-eight miles east across the bay. In the spring of 1914, trains of flatcars loaded with hundreds of palm trees arrived on the Jewel City's tracks. The legions of Canary Island date palms (*Phoenix canariensis*) and California fan palms (*Washingtonia filifera*), leaning backward to protect them from the winds of travel, appeared to lounge indolently against one another.

After each specimen was transferred to a wagon, teams of eight powerful draft horses pulled it into position, the taller date palms alternating every twenty feet with the smaller, fuller fan palms. For added tropical effect, McLaren planted passion vines at the base of the trees. These twined up the trunks and dropped festoons of brilliant flowers from the branches.

As San Franciscans well know, it's nearly impossible to grow oranges in the foggy city with its sometimes-biting winds. Fully aware of this, McLaren planned one last feat using the delicate citrus trees. He had more than one hundred mature orange trees grown in the more benevolent climate of Cloverdale, about seventy-six miles north of the city, and sideboxed them using the same innovative method as he had for the other transplanted trees. He waited until December 1914, just two months before the exposition opened, then brought them to the fair with their fruit carefully tied and protected. Only two of these verdant, ten-foot-high, eight-foot-diameter trees would fit on each railroad car.

The orange trees were arrayed, still in their boxes, in orderly rows about architect Louis Christian Mullgardt's opulent Court of Ages, where they evoked the courtyards of Moorish Andalusia. Those who had visited the palaces of southern Spain recognized the

Main Entrance, Pan. Pac. Int. Expo., San Francisco.

influences of the Aljafería, the forecourt of the Great Mosque of Córdoba, and the Patio de los Naranjos of the Seville Cathedral. All through the spring of 1915, those taking their evening stroll around the great Fountain of Earth in the calm, sheltered Court of Ages were greeted by the sweet scent of orange blossoms and ripe fruit.

The most talked-about feature of the grounds was undoubtedly the wall of living greenery that served as the boundary of the Jewel City for nearly a quarter of a mile (1,150 feet) along the Chestnut Street façade of the exposition. Most of the wall stood twenty feet tall, but at the Main Entrance at Scott Street, it shot upward above the turnstiles into nine exuberant arches, each thirty-six feet high.

Since no ordinary hedge could have been grown with such speed, size, or perfection, McLaren's sorcery again was on display. To create the looming green barrier, he ordered a small, magenta-colored ice plant variety (*Mesembryanthemum spectabilis*). These were planted in 8,700 large, flat trays—each six feet long, two feet wide, and filled with soil two and a half inches deep. The fronts of the trays were enclosed with wire mesh, creating a building unit of freely growing ice plant that would not lose its form when eventually mounted vertically. The plants grew quite abundantly in the trays, which were placed on the ground beside the Palace of Horticulture while their future framework was assembled along the façade of the fair.

Opposite, Above: Court of Ages landscaped with orange trees. Opposite, Below: Postcard of John McLaren's remarkable ice plant hedge fence, with thirty-foot tall arches at the Exposition's main entrance. Below: The Palace of Fine Arts is one of the remaining architectural remnants from the 1915 Exposition.

When the ice plant was mature, the trays were affixed to the tall wooden armature, which consisted of two parallel walls eight feet apart, lending an illusion of thick solidity to the wall. Based on meteorological conditions, the fence would be brushed with flecks of gauzy, pink color, contrasting against the background of the dark green succulent foliage. The Hedge Fence was a huge hit, though fairgoers were left wondering how it was done.

The remarkable effects McLaren achieved reflect his ingenuity and mastery of the arts and sciences of horticulture and landscape design. "To John McLaren, nothing is impossible," declared the *New York Tribune*. Shortly after the Jewel City's closure in 1916, a *San Francisco Chronicle* headline asserted, "John McLaren's Work at the Exposition Entitles Him to the Name of Magic Gardener."[6] Yet the ever-taciturn, self-effacing chief of landscape declined credit, saying at a Commonwealth Club luncheon where his work was lauded, "The California climate did it. We just looked on."[7]

# MARION HOLLINS AND THE CREATION OF THE PASATIEMPO GOLF CLUB IN SANTA CRUZ

Desmond Smith

Pasatiempo was the brainchild of Marion Hollins. It would have represented the crowning achievement of her remarkable career but for its timing. The golf course opened to great acclaim in September 1929, fifty-one days before the Wall Street crash.

Born into a wealthy family on Long Island (her financier father was a friend and associate of J.P. Morgan), Marion grew up alongside four older male siblings—which may have explained her competitive spirit. An outstanding athlete, she excelled at several sports: golf (she won the US Women's Amateur Title in 1921), polo and steeplechasing, tennis, marksman-

ship, and motor racing. She was widely regarded as the best all-round sportswoman of the 1920s. Her entrepreneurial gifts were in early evidence when she cofounded and developed the Women's National Golf and Tennis Club on Long Island, the first all-female golf club. As preparation for this project, she traveled to Britain to research the design and operation of the best golf courses.

Below: From left, Cyril J.H. Tolley, Marion Hollins, Bobby Jones, and Glenna Collette, opening day at Pasatiempo. Opposite: Aerial of Pasatiempo Golf Course.

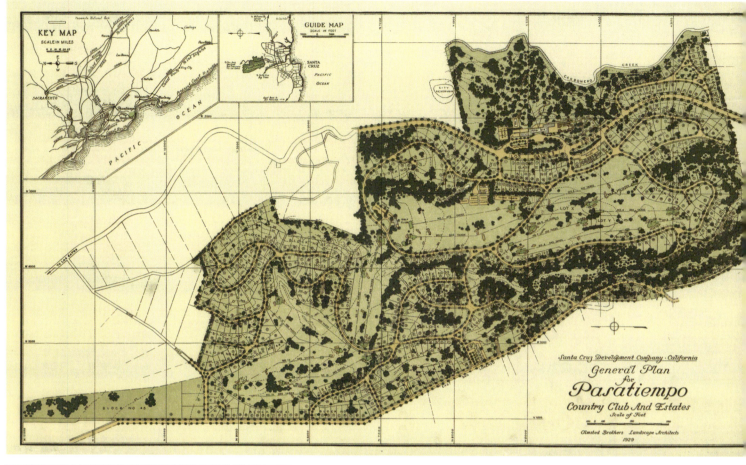

CALIFORNIA EDEN

In 1925, Hollins teamed with Samuel Morse, owner of much of the Monterey Peninsula (formerly the Del Monte Estates), who was in the process of developing what would become the world's most renowned golfing destination. He recruited her as athletics director of Pebble Beach. Since this position included organizing tournaments and attracting new members and potential purchasers to the resort, her extensive social network among the wealthy and famous proved invaluable. With Morse's backing, she was responsible in 1928 for the creation of the exclusive Cypress Point Club, gloriously situated on the picturesque Monterey coast.

Her next and most ambitious project was a 570-acre site (formerly the Rancho Carbonera) in the hills above Santa Cruz. She called it Pasatiempo, Spanish for "hobby" or "pastime." Her vision was to create her own planned community complex that would rival Pebble Beach. The centerpiece would be the golf course, but the compound would include polo fields, a racetrack, bridal paths, a marina, and swimming pools, with multiple housing lots and a hotel.

As always, Hollins showed an uncanny flair for picking talent. Her choice for golf course architect was Alister MacKenzie with whom she had collaborated in the design of Cypress Point. He is now recognized as one of the game's greatest architects, noted especially for courses that are fair to players of all levels of ability, and for his skill in making artificial landforms appear to be natural.

Initially, Hollins had wanted Duncan McDuffie of Mason McDuffie to coordinate the project. His experience with the development of large-scale residential projects made him well qualified for the role. He declined her offer, citing other commitments, but strongly recommended she speak with James "Fred" Dawson, principal of the West Coast office of Olmsted Brothers. Coincidentally, it turned out that Dawson had already worked for Hollins's parents some years before on their family estate at Islip, Long Island. Given this history and the immediate rapport between them, Hollins hired the Olmsted firm as the master planners for the project. Later, she commissioned architects Clarence Tantau to design the clubhouse and guesthouse, and a youthful William Wurster to design her own house on the property. Thomas Church, the supervising landscape architect, had both his home and studio on site.

Despite the collapse of the stock market and warnings of further economic recession, Hollins remained optimistic and pressed ahead with her plans. In the early years of the 1930s, Pasatiempo was a playground for the rich and famous, notably the Hollywood set. Ultimately, however, the length and depth of the Depression having exhausted her personal fortune and borrowings, she was forced to sell Pasatiempo to her creditors in 1940. Moreover, a serious car crash three years earlier, in which she was struck head-on by a drunk driver, had left her with brain damage and precipitated her decline. She died of cancer in 1942.

While Hollins had a short life, her legacy continues. Pasatiempo (now restored) and Cypress Point golf course, her most admired course, survive and are much acclaimed for the quality of their concept, location, and design. Hollins and MacKenzie are celebrated as the joint creators of these two outstanding places. Recent research suggests that Bobby Jones, the Tiger Woods of his era, in his original concept for Augusta National (home of the Masters Tournament in Atlanta) derived much of his inspiration from Hollins's work at Cypress and Pasatiempo. So great was his admiration, he also used MacKenzie and Olmsted Brothers.

In 2022, Marion Hollins was inducted into the World Golf Hall of Fame in belated recognition of her unique contribution to the history of the sport and her visionary role in creating several iconic golfing venues. As a woman working in a world dominated by men, her achievements in golf are unrivaled to this day.

Above: Portrait of Dr. Alister MacKenzie during his early career as a doctor before becoming a golf course architect. Opposite, Above: Olmsted Brothers' design for Santa Cruz Development Company, California, General Plan for Pasatiempo Country Club. Opposite, Below: View at Fourteenth Green, Pasatiempo Country Club, Santa Cruz. Overleaf: Men and women playing on Eighteenth Green, Pasatiempo Country Club, Santa Cruz.

# ANZA-BORREGO DESERT STATE PARK

Lee Somerville

East of the city of San Diego, mountainous roads pass through historic towns that highlight early settlement and the development of agriculture and tourism in the culturally and topographically diverse county of San Diego. These mountain roads lead to the largest and possibly the most ecologically important desert landscape in the entire United States. At 585,000 acres, Anza-Borrego Desert State Park composes one-fifth of San Diego County, extending into Riverside County to the north and Imperial County to the east. Geologically, the park forms the northern rim of the rift valley of the ancient Gulf of California, making it an area rich in fossil-bearing sediment and unique topography including badlands, desert plains, natural springs with palm oases, and dry washes. The higher,

northern edge of the park falls within the California montane ecosystem, but the valley floor is part of the Colorado Desert ecosystem, resulting in a wide variety of flora and fauna within the confines of the park.

Opposite: Indigenous Cahuilla people in the region traditionally harvested the fruits of the California fan palm and used its fronds for basketry and fiber. Today there are numerous Cahuilla Bands of Indians living in San Diego, Riverside, and Imperial counties. Below: The Borrego Badlands were uplifted and then eroded by wind and water. Fossils indicate that one or two million years ago, sabertooth cats, mastodons, and camels lived here. Overleaf: Mature and young native California fan palms (*Washingtonia filifera*) on the Borrego Palm Canyon Trail where a natural spring permits their growth. As the blackened trunks on the mature palms indicate, they quickly recover from fires.

The area was recognized as an important desert landscape by explorers and environmentalists in the late nineteenth century, but it was not until 1928 that Borrego Palms Desert State Park, at the time comprising about two hundred thousand acres, was founded. (*Borrego* is the Spanish word for the bighorn sheep that inhabit the area, and *palms* in the name refers to the native California fan palm, *Washingtonia filifera*, found in abundance here.) In 1932, the expanded park was renamed the Anza-Borrego Desert State Park to honor Spanish explorer Juan Bautista de Anza, who led expeditions in the late eighteenth century from Spanish colonial Mexico and Arizona, then part of New Spain, across this desert to San Francisco. The route he established for settlers is now designated a National Historic Trail.

The rocky history of the park's establishment included political and financial conflicts over land acquisition, ownership, and proposed development that lasted for many years. Minerva Hamilton Hoyt of Pasadena was an early advocate for protecting California deserts, especially Joshua Tree, Borrego Palms, and Death Valley. The final successful outcome for Anza-Borrego was largely due to the ongoing concern and commitment of a group of San Diego philanthropists, including George Marston and Ellen Browning Scripps, who not only donated land and provided financial assistance but also clearly understood the importance of preserving this significant cultural landscape for future generations.

The park's visitor center in Borrego Springs is a great starting point for exploration of the physical and cultural history of the region, and a well-labeled pathway through a demonstration area highlights the commonly seen plants and cacti in the park. With twelve wilderness areas and over one hundred miles of hiking trails, the park offers many opportunities for exploration. There are two not-to-be-missed walks. One is up Borrego Palm Canyon, where, at the end of the trail, a grove of the endangered native California fan palms suddenly materializes in a cool oasis with a natural spring. The second one begins with a drive along the four-mile unpaved road to Font's Point. Once there, you can walk the length of the crest and gaze at the expanse of the desert floor, while the shadows lengthen and change on the peaks and valleys of the badlands. While the park may seem entirely natural, there are traces of the Cahuilla Indians, old mines, and former ranch lands as well as carefully designed paved and unpaved roads, trails, campgrounds, and scenic viewpoints in this cultural landscape.

This desert is full of interesting flora. In addition to many locations where springs and subsurface water permit the growth of California fan palms, the strangely contorted elephant tree (*Bursera microphylla*) grows here, as do smoke trees (*Psorothamnus spinosus*), agaves, barrel cactus, indigo bush, desert lavender, and ocotillo. During a rainy year in the spring blooming season, usually in February and March, visitors might experience a superbloom—an almost magical array of color and texture in the delicate flowers of the desert floor. Thanks to the perceptive individuals who worked so hard to preserve this natural habitat and dynamic landscape, future generations can experience the beauty of the desert and its star-filled night skies.

Above Left: A "superbloom" of spring wildflowers often follows a wet winter season in the desert. Different areas feature different species of colorful flowers. Above Right: Indigo-colored blossoms of the smoke tree (*Psorothamnus spinosus*). These shrubby, grey trees bloom briefly in spring and only grow in canyon washes where there are flash floods. Opposite: Prickly-pear cactus (*Opuntia* spp.) has edible fruits, and the type of century plant known as desert agave or mescal (*Agave deserti var. deserti* in the background) was an important source of food and fiber for the Indigenous people of the region. Its blossoms attract hummingbirds, bats, and bees.

# LAPD'S ROCK GARDEN

Phoebe Cutler

The cascade, in its multivarious forms, became widespread in large estate gardens in the United States during the 1920s and 1930s. In Los Angeles, silent film stars Harold Llyod and Buster Keaton, oil man Edward L. Doheny, and Packard dealer Earl Anthony count among the well-healed clientele who capped their yards with stepped water courses. Scattered across Los Angeles—and dotted even more thickly in Santa Barbara and Pasadena—these water features drew their inspiration from Italian Renaissance masterworks on the order of Villa d'Este and Villa Lante. Strangely enough, one of the last and grandest was conceived and constructed by the Los Angeles Police Department. In the mid-1930s, Chief James E. Davis resolved that the Los Angeles Police Revolver and Athletic Club (LAPRAAC), located in Elysian Park, needed a cascade. Appropriate to the bucolic setting, Davis opted for the rustic, rock garden version of the water chain. Lacking the suitable rocks, he was fortunate to have at hand an expert in the art of artificial stonework.

Police presence in Elysian Park dated back to the crime-ridden days of Prohibition. In the early 1920s, a surge in the construction of shooting ranges followed close on the heels of a nationwide push for better marksmanship. Los Angeles followed suit with a range and a corresponding pistol club housed in a building that had been a dormitory for the 1932 Olympics. The stimulus for a rock garden arose from

the decision, in 1935, to relocate all police training to the park, which is set in the wider embrace of Chavez Ravine. A fundraiser was held to support the vision of "terraces, cascades, rock gardens, and trout ponds," in a word, a venue that would complement the dual functions of training and recreation. Davis then approached the city's Parks Commission to gain its approval and support.[1]

Meanwhile, three miles away, at Seventh Street and South Broadway, an adventurous restaurateur, Clifford Clinton, was preparing Clifton's Brookdale, a standout among the many themed eateries of the day and the second in his chain of Clifton's Cafeterias. In the main dining room, the patrons would be surrounded by boulders that formed waterfalls, cascades, a fireplace, and a grotto. Above them would rise fabricated redwoods, while a stream would run by their tables. This tour de force, inspired by a historic Santa Cruz County restaurant, was an immediate success among a wide spectrum of Angelenos. Indeed, it is

Below Left: Clifton's Brookdale Cafeteria musicians surrounded by forest scenes on "Melody Ledge" atop the artificial rockwork created by François Scotti. Below Right: The St. Francis Fountain at the base of Mount Rubidoux in Riverside, California, was another creation by François Scotti. Opposite: The LAPD Rock Garden was the baby of 1930s Police Chief James E. Davis ("Two-Gun" Davis) who here poses proudly with his achievement.

not too much to venture that Clifton's was the inspiration for the Chavez Ravine "terraces, cascades, rock gardens, and trout ponds," not least because Davis proceeded to engage the very same craftsman who created that cafeteria's fanciful settings.[2]

François Scotti represented the third generation of a rock garden business based in the French Riviera. One of the triumphs of Scotti's "Casa Rustica" business was a structure in Monte Carlo. Although the identity of the work has been lost, this faux rock extravaganza inspired two unrelated North American tourists key to this narrative. The first of the two, Robert Butchart, a Canadian cement manufacturer, proceeded, in 1910, to import the son of the landmark's creators to his home near Victoria, British Columbia, to stay for a year to teach his ancestral skills and to contribute some garden accessories. In this way, Butchart sought to embellish his eponymous—and still celebrated—landmark with rustic concrete fencing, pergolas, and other features.

After a year of employment in Victoria, Scotti moved to Los Angeles where he initially struggled but then was able to compile an impressive portfolio of work. In 1915 alone, he completed two very visible projects: an agriculture display, presumably for the new State Exposition Building in Exposition Park, and an unspecified work for the Panama-California Exposition in San Diego. As with the mysterious feature in Monte Carlo, the latter is unknown and possibly no longer extant. Yet, while it existed, the San Diego creation incited Charles M. Loring, considered the founder of the Minneapolis Park system, to engage Scotti to erect the still-extant shrine to Saint Francis at the foot of Mount Rubidoux in Riverside, Loring's winter home. The Mount Rubidoux rockery is in

three parts: a steep waterfall on the left, a central area of large boulders encasing a tribute to Saint Francis, and a large cavern on the right. The outsized stonework runs the gamut from round to square to sheer. Planting is minimal and concentrated in the middle. The overall effect is chaotic, unlike the controlled layering of largely flat boulders in the Elysian Park cascade, where planting greatly enhances the faux rockwork. The successful and civic-minded midwestern entrepreneur—the second of our impressionable tourists—was dumbfounded when he learned that the Los Angeles artist he had commissioned was, in fact, the scion of the French Riviera masons whose work he had admired years ago in Monaco.

For the generous donor of the Rubidoux shrine, the cascade was an unmitigated success. Loring proceeded to engage Scotti to produce a forty-foot-high version for a park in Minneapolis. That now-defunct work more closely predicted what the sculptor would do some twenty years later. The rocks, although still sizable boulders, were flatter and more homogeneous. The waterfall became, like the LAPRAAC cascade, central to the composition. Expressing his admiration for the work, Theodore Wirth, the contemporary park superintendent in Minnesota, commented that you could not tell that the rockwork was not natural to the geology of the area.

In between the Rubidoux and Loring cascades and Clifton's Brookdale's elaborate set design, Scotti had been advancing his craft. He explained in a letter to Robert Butchart that after much experimentation he had developed "new formulas" that "will enable me to produce on a much larger scale." Accelerated production would, indeed, be critical to the ultimate success of the commission in Elysian Park.[3]

Above Left: The LAPD Rock Garden's principal cascade, as viewed to the east from the lower terrace. This being Los Angeles, Tarzan more than once flew over this waterfall and its flanking stairs in movies. Above Right: Mid-section of the cascade showing the amphitheater, piers with traces of Scotti's coloration, and some of the lush planting palette.

The full scope of Scotti's work is unknown, but without knowing it, one might still nominate the carefully crafted LAPRAAC Rock Garden as his chef d'oeuvre. It was a remarkable merger of diffuse planting, falling water, and artificial rock. The steepness and scale of the raw site—about four hundred feet wide and sixty feet high, with an approximate twenty-degree rise—added to its stature. Conceived as a relaxing retreat for the members of the police force and their families, at the base of the cascade was a forty-foot-deep patio, which, at one time contained a trout pond. Movies were screened in the garden, and a barbecue was tucked into a rock ledge in the southeast corner.

Constructed by off-duty policemen who were members of the pistol club, the rock garden rose in a sequence of six additional levels with a total of four pools. At the center of the entry terrace, water spilled over a pair of ledges into a terminal basin. Twin walls draped with greenery protruded on either side of the pool. Coved seats, also concrete, bracketed the walls, while a matching pair of stairs led to the next level. Here the garden took on a new character, opening out into a larger pool and an amphitheater-like space. Three tiers of narrow seating flanked a third, central waterfall. The planting scheme, the work of an unknown artist, was originally well tended and luxuriant with pines and bamboo defining spaces. Azalea, camellia, sword fern, asparagus fern, and photinia emerged from pockets in the rocks. Three rock piers were equally dramatic. These piers rose from the semicircle layering of faux rock that backed up the tiered seating embracing the central rill.

Another pool and two more narrow cascades took visitors to a fourth level, where a brick walk led past a semicircular wall, a grotto, and two soaring banana specimens. Furthering the chromatic effect, the ivy-draped wall was made of concrete blocks accented with large sandstone slabs. Similarly accented walls encircled the next two and final levels. The top layer included seating nooks, or hemicycles, classical features that, along with the twin stairways and the loosely symmetrical composition, speak to the European origins of this rock fantasy. At this level, a modern intrusion—a panoramic view of downtown Los Angeles—at once elevates and grounds the visitor.

The *Los Angeles Police Department Annual Report, 1936–1937* hailed the "simulated sandstone strata, artistically designed to produce changing color effects as suggested by the Grand Canyon." The southwestern influence explains the flatness of the layers of rock and the relative smoothness of their surface, as well as the overall rose coloring. Where dark iron tones appear, especially in the water channels, it could be just the staining of time, but it could also be the enhancing of Scotti's original intent. As testimony to that intent, a bronze plaque set in the patio at the base of the falls reads, "Concrete Rockcraft and Chemical Coloring, Francois Scotti, Los Angeles, CA." Scotti died in 1959.

Despite being named a Los Angeles Historic-Cultural Monument in 1973, the LAPD Rock Garden and its planting fell into disrepair. The cascade and pools were being renovated at the time of this writing, and there have been revisions to the original design. People can still access the rock garden through a tunnel adjacent to the police clubhouse, where both police and members of the public can purchase breakfast and lunch. The garden is advertised on the LAPRAAC website as "the perfect place for Retirements, Reunions, and Weddings."[4]

Above Left: Francois Scotti, the virtuoso behind the LAPD Rock Garden, poses in front of his sculpted work in the garden at Clifton's Pacific Seas location, 1939. Above Right: With its rock work, fountain, and planting, the design of this new plaza seems to pay tribute to Scotti's original rock garden, which is located through the tunnel to the left and is currently being renovated.

# GARRETT ECKBO'S FULTON MALL

Harold Tokmakian and H. Ray McKnight

Fulton Mall, a historic, pedestrian-only shopping area in downtown Fresno, was an urban park filled with trees, shrubs, fountains, and sculptures, which came under threat beginning in 2002.[1] The city administration strenuously attempted to eliminate it, despite a deficiency of parkland and green space in Fresno. No matter that in the Trust for Public Land's rankings of the park systems of the forty largest American cities, Fresno came in last, while San Francisco, Sacramento, and New York were the top three.[2]

The origin and fate of Fulton Mall was closely linked with Fresno's growth over the past several decades. As its population rapidly increased, reaching one hundred thousand in 1958, Fresno expanded in many areas. Education, health, and retail services began to follow Fresno State College's relocation from central Fresno to a site several miles to the northeast. Manchester Center, Fresno's first regional shopping center, was built to the north of the downtown area. The chamber of commerce, city hall, and business property owners became concerned about the downtown's viability as the center of retail shopping, health care, and government. The Redevelopment Agency of the City of Fresno was created and began to lay the groundwork to clear blight from downtown with the cooperation of merchants and property owners. An organization called the "100 Percenters" formed to collaborate with the city in the search for a solution, and in 1958 architect and urban designer Victor Gruen was hired to propose an urban revitalization plan for downtown Fresno.

Already known for his plan for Fort Worth, Texas, Gruen was asked to apply similar design concepts to Fresno. In less than two years, the Central Area Plan emerged. The plan consisted of three elements: an auto-free core retail superblock surrounded by a one-way street loop, a freeway loop around the central area, and dense housing to support the commercial base. The centerpiece of the central core was to be the transformation of six blocks of Fulton Street, the city's traditional retail center, into a pedestrian mall. Gruen's plan was approved in 1960, and reconstruction work began.

Gruen had the foresight to engage Garrett Eckbo, a world-renowned landscape architect, to design the

Below Left: Undated portrait of landscape architect Garrett Eckbo. Below Right: Image from "The Gruen Plan" for the Fresno central area. This image provided a vision of Fulton Street after traffic was removed and landscape features were added. Opposite: Garrett Eckbo laid out the hardscape design in a pattern to symbolize the Central Valley's soil color and contours.

pedestrian mall. Born in California and educated at the University of California, Berkeley, and the Harvard Graduate School of Design, Eckbo was a leading practitioner and theoretician of modernist mid-twentieth-century landscape architecture and author of the 1950 publication *Landscape for Living*.

After years of designing gardens for private homes in Southern California, Eckbo began receiving commissions for larger projects—planned communities, college campuses, and parks. Beginning with his student years at Harvard, Eckbo developed an untraditional design aesthetic that rejected the usual opposition between informal garden style and the symmetry of Beaux Arts style. Two basic components of Eckbo's aesthetic can be summarized as "the organic principle" and "the social principle." The organic principle rejected the notion that design begins with a preconceived concept and arrangement. Instead, design and arrangement should grow out of a place, capturing its genius loci.

Eckbo's organic vision for Fulton Mall was to capture various aspects of the San Joaquin Valley, especially its topography and agriculture. The mall's concrete pavement was stained an adobe color to denote the soil of the San Joaquin Valley. Ribbons of unstained concrete aggregate eight and a half inches wide, sometimes gently curving and sometimes angular, ran across the pavement at frequent intervals, suggesting the contours of the valley floor while also contributing to the rhythmic unity of the mall.

A variety of water features throughout the mall symbolized the importance of water in the San Joaquin Valley. Water falling from one level to another in multilevel pools and into curving streams or straight channels alluded to the movement of water from the Sierras into the valley's rivers and irrigation canals. The twenty-six sculpted ceramic pipes that were part of the water features represented the standpipes that are common to agricultural irrigation systems. And interspersed throughout the mall were 144 trees and a large number of shrubs and flowers in planting beds of many shapes, sizes, and elevations.

Inspired by the art of Joan Miró, Jean Arp, and Wassily Kandinsky, Eckbo gave the planters and water features curving, biomorphic forms: shapes that reflected the organic principle. He chose the original plantings from a list of plant materials appropriate for the valley that the Fresno Parks and Recreation Department compiled at his request. Eckbo completed his vision of a harmonious whole by integrating sculpture into the landscape design, creating an outdoor museum. Civic-minded citizens donated the nineteen sculptures by renowned artists that enhanced the beauty of the mall. Charles Birnbaum, founder and president of the Cultural Landscape Foundation, noted

Above Left: A water feature through the Mall alluded to the movement of water from the Sierras to the Valley through use of biomorphic forms, 2008. Fountain entitled "Obos" was designed by George Tsutakawa. Above Right: Like many of the original art pieces, water feature "Dancing Waters" by Stan Bitters was preserved when the mall was returned to two-way vehicular traffic in 2016.

that the large display of contemporary art by recognized local and international artists was an early, if not the first, sculpture garden outside of a museum.

Eckbo explained how the social principle was applied in Fulton Mall in *People in a Landscape*, a book he published with coauthors Laura Lawson, Walter Hood, and Chip Sullivan in 1998. In the chapter "Fresno Downtown Mall, Fresno, California," he stated that the mall "was designed as and has become a social space, a focus of community interest and events, a promenade and rendezvous with friends, a play area for children, and a meeting place for teenagers."[3]

The mall was certainly a people place: an outdoor stage for social interaction for the city's diverse population to comfortably visit friends, observe others, shop, sit, play, and relax in downtown Fresno. This goal was achieved with eighty seating areas of various sizes and configurations, eighteen of which contained benches with brightly colored mosaic backs. Other seating

areas were circular platforms fourteen feet in diameter and two feet above ground level, surrounded by low plantings. While these platforms provided isolated spaces of respite separated from the flow of pedestrian traffic, they were also vista points for observing the scenery and passersby. A play area for children anchored each end of the mall.

In September 1964, the ribbon was cut, and the six blocks of Fulton Mall and short sections of transecting streets were opened to pedestrians. The fountains flowed and the planters were bright with color. Fresno families enjoyed this special occasion along with local and state officials, including Governor Edmund G. ("Pat") Brown. The mall quickly gained worldwide recognition as a masterwork merging sculpture with landscape architecture. It immediately gave Fresno an identity, a sense of place. Visitors from other parts of the country and other parts of the world came to enjoy a place worth seeing. Gruen and Eckbo gave Fresno a gift, a unique urban park with all its elements harmoniously integrated.

Fulton Mall's success in maintaining downtown Fresno as a retail center, however, was short-lived. Beginning in 1974, the City of Fresno began to follow a general plan policy of decentralization that allowed the creation of one regional shopping center after

another as part of a residential northward sprawl. The city failed to create a concentration of housing in the central area, an important component of the Gruen plan. Another component of the Gruen plan, building a freeway loop around the central area, was delayed for many years. As retail business declined downtown, there were some who chose not to recognize unfortunate planning decisions as the cause, but instead made Fulton Mall the scapegoat. Their solution was to return auto traffic to the pedestrian mall. In 2002, in the first concerted effort to achieve this goal, a design firm chosen by the Redevelopment Agency presented a plan to the city council. Their scheme was to remove most of the trees and fountains and force the relocation or destruction of most of the sculptures, thus destroying Fulton Mall as a quiet meeting place and urban park. The large outpouring of public opposition, supported by many business owners, persuaded the city council to abandon the plan.

Leading the opposition to the proposal to destroy the mall was the Downtown Fresno Coalition, a group of citizens who organized for the express purpose of maintaining and preserving Fulton Mall and other open spaces in the downtown area. The group determined that since Fulton Mall was a unique landscape designed by a master landscape architect, and a place of national and global significance, it must be considered for the National Register of Historic Places. Without any support from the city administration, the group prepared the nomination. After learning that the National Register nomination was being given serious consideration by the California Office of Historic Preservation, the City of Fresno asked for a delay. Enlisting the opposition of most of the owners of properties adjacent to the mall, the city administration made a concerted effort to prevent the listing of the mall in the National Register. In August 2010, the National Park Service determined Fulton Mall eligible for listing in the National Register of Historic Places, which automatically placed the mall in the California Register of Historical Resources. The announcement by the National Park Service confirmed the significance of the mall for the collaborative efforts of Victor Gruen and Garrett Eckbo in helping define modern urban design and planning.

Rejecting the opportunity to capitalize on this recognition of Fulton Mall as a historical resource worthy of promotion, the city administration appeared determined to tear up the mall to make way for automobiles, claiming that this would magically turn the downtown into a shopping mecca. This view ignored the fact that Fulton Street was beginning to fail as a retail center in the early 1960s as businesses moved north to Manchester Center and elsewhere. Perhaps more importantly, it was a view that refused to acknowledge the broad support among citizens for preserving Fulton Mall. The strong opposition to vehicularizing the mall shown in 2002 has been demonstrated at various times since then. In 2006, the city council called for a study of Fulton Mall so that a

decision could be made about its future. A study group consisting mostly of city employees was chosen, and two professional facilitators conducted a series of public meetings to garner citizen opinion. The facilitators compiled a list of themes that emerged from the meetings, and at the head of that list was "No traffic on the mall." This clear expression of support for saving the mall was the probable reason for the shelving of the study group's report.

During the years of ongoing debate about the fate of Fulton Mall, the city did not consistently maintain it, and the neglect was acutely observable. Some water features were empty. The once lush and beautiful flower beds lost much of their luster. Pavement cleaning and repair was infrequent. Fulton Mall showed a shameful lack of municipal stewardship. The latest effort to put traffic on the mall was reaching a critical juncture. From 2010 to 2013, the City of Fresno conducted yet another study, this time to produce a Fulton Corridor Specific Plan (FCSP) as part of an effort to revitalize Fresno's downtown. A citizens' committee was appointed to propose a draft FCSP to be presented to the city council, including three options for Fulton Mall. The committee included two versions of returning vehicular traffic to the mall, though the main difference between the two was the degree to which Eckbo's design would be destroyed. The first option left little or nothing of Eckbo's design. The second option, energetically advocated by the city as the mayor's choice, claimed to include an effort to save portions of the mall—words like *vignette* were frequently used—but would nevertheless shatter the integrity of Eckbo's design.

Fifty years post-construction, Fulton Mall became an established historical resource. When it opened, the mall was emblematic of the free-flowing creativity and optimism of 1960s urban design, and of a city that valued its residents—and with Eckbo's design, a true landscape for living.

Despite the historical and cultural value of Fulton Mall, in what was determined to be a revitalization of downtown Fresno, Fulton Mall was demolished in 2016 and returned to the two-way vehicular Fulton Street. According to then-mayor Ashley Swearengin, "Downtown is poised for a renaissance and we hope that these new businesses opening now will one day become iconic—restoring Fulton Street as the heart of the downtown. My strong belief is that ten years from now downtown and Fulton Street will be transformed into a more vibrant and prosperous destination."[4] The sculptures were moved to Fresno's Kern Plaza.

One of eight mosaic benches on Fulton Mall, designed by Joyce Aiken and Jean Ray Laury, originally built in 1964, with each having a different mosaic design. The wood bench materials were later replaced with coated metal elements.

# MID-CENTURY MODERN

## THE KAISER ROOF GARDEN COMES OF AGE

Marlea A. Graham

In 2010, Oakland's Kaiser Roof Garden turned fifty years old, qualifying the landscape to become a National Historic Landmark. This garden was the brainchild of California industrialist Henry J. Kaiser. Kaiser intended that Kaiser Center Inc. serve as the headquarters of his international business empire and a highly visible symbol of his impact on the business world, particularly in California. Though *Forbes* magazine once ranked Kaiser as the eleventh most influential industrialist of all time, today he is largely unknown to younger generations except as the namesake of Kaiser Permanente.

A native of New York state, Kaiser had relocated to California by 1906. He began in the construction business, entering his industrial phase during World War II. By the 1950s, his influence on Californians' lives was pervasive. One could live in a Kaiser-built house equipped with Kaiser-brand appliances, drive to work in a Kaiser automobile on Kaiser-built roads and bridges, and, if injured en route or on the job, be treated at a Kaiser hospital. By the time of Kaiser's death, Kaiser Industries Corporation consisted of some ninety Kaiser-affiliated companies and subsidiaries. When Kaiser decided it was time to build his corporate headquarters, Oakland was his city of choice. He acquired the campus of the College of the Holy Names in 1955; its Lake Merritt view was the perfect setting for his corporate palace. Construction began in 1959.

Why did Kaiser want a roof garden on top of the parking garage adjacent to his office tower? In his first published article about the garden in *Landscape Architecture*, landscape architect Theodore Osmundson wrote that this was merely following a fixed Kaiser policy of "good housekeeping." "The three and one-half acre garage roof...could not be left a concrete desert to be abhorred by the viewers from the offices in the tower and the surrounding office buildings of downtown

Above: Aerial view of the Kaiser Roof Garden showing biomorphic layout within Oakland's urban context, c. 1960s. Left: Pools and planting areas were designed in undulating curves in a lush planting.

Oakland. It was decided to make this roof a semi-public park."[1] However, newspaper articles of the day make it clear that the City Planning Commission also played a role in this decision. When Osmundson's book, *Roof Gardens: History, Design, and Construction*, was released in 1999, the *San Francisco Examiner*'s book reviewer had Osmundson incorrectly naming Kaiser's son Edgar as the guiding force behind the garden, influenced by his exposure during the war years to the roof gardens of Rockefeller Center. Kaiser's Fifth Avenue offices did overlook Rockefeller Center's famous ice-skating rink and restaurant, but it was Henry who frequently availed himself of recreational breaks on the rink. Former top Kaiser executive Cornell Maier recalled stories told to him by Edgar Kaiser and another Kaiser executive, Eugene E. Trefethen, reiterating that the garden was all Henry's idea. "He wanted a roof garden. Everybody

tried to talk him out of it. They said 'It's not practical to have a garden on top of a garage. It's expensive, a lot of weight. You'd have to have extra steel and so forth. If he hadn't persisted I don't think we would have had a roof garden.'"[2]

The parallels between Rockefeller and Kaiser Center are clear, and it was always Henry Kaiser who pushed for these similarities, wanting a roof garden with an ice-skating rink, a posh restaurant, and high-class department store at Kaiser Center to bring in the downtown shoppers. Some early promotional literature for Kaiser Center actually referred to it as Rockefeller Center West. When Henry Kaiser left California in 1955 for new challenges in Hawaii, he placed Edgar at the head of Kaiser Industries and made Alonzo B. Ordway the center's project manager, but interoffice memos clearly show that Kaiser Sr. still had the controlling hand, paying frequent visits back to oversee the work on building and garden.

Certainly, Edgar was instrumental in seeing the garden completed and in maintaining it over the years that Kaiser Industries remained owners of the property. It was Edgar who recommended hiring the firm of Osmundson & Staley to design and install the roof garden, noting that he had personal experience of their skills. David Arbegast, then an associate member of Osmundson & Staley, noted that Edgar had hired the firm in 1955 to landscape his estate in Lafayette, Contra Costa County.[3]

Osmundson earned his degree in landscape architecture from Iowa State College in 1943. Soon thereafter, he moved to California, where he worked briefly, in turn, for both Thomas Church and Garrett Eckbo. Classmate John H. Staley Jr. also earned his degree in 1943 and served in the US Army before taking up graduate studies at the University of California, Berkeley. In 1946, Osmundson, Staley, and a third classmate, Jack Gibson, combined forces, but by 1949, the firm was reduced to Osmundson & Staley, remain-

Far Left: Henry J. Kaiser. Left: Theodore Osmundson. Osmundson & Staley included partner John H. Staley Jr. and then associate member David Arbegast. Below: Landscape architect John Sue's custom-designed water feature using Kaiser cement. The biomorphic curves, concrete planters, and exposed aggregate paving are all typical of Modernist gardens. Center: The legs of these clean, simple, Modernist white benches continue the site's curvilinear forms. Opposite: A drawing showing the complex construction for tree installation on the roof, showing the drainage system.

ing partners until 1965. Their working styles complemented each other. Osmundson excelled at political and social networking, public relations, finding clients, and keeping them happy, while Staley supervised design and construction. In 1956, the firm had enough work to justify hiring David Arbegast, yet another Iowa State graduate with a master's from UC Berkeley, who drew up the final design for the Kaiser garden.

While the garden is considered significant for its association with Henry J. Kaiser, it is also significant for being the largest contiguous roof garden in the world when it opened to the public in 1960. It is one of the few surviving gardens designed by Osmundson & Staley for a commercial client, and a relatively well-preserved icon of the mid-century modern style. It was, in its heyday, perhaps the best example found in the United States of a roof garden of the intensive style, with parklike features.

Despite Kaiser's expressed wishes, Ordway kept turning down design ideas in hopes the garden would just go away. Arbegast recalled, "We did at least twenty schemes for that building. And Mr. Ordway would always reject them because [he] did not want the garden. The way it finally ended up was that he asked for a couple more drawings. I made them and Ted took them over there and [Ordway] said, 'We'll build that one.' No discussion. 'We'll build that one.' We'd gotten three there and naturally I didn't like the one he chose at all."[4]

Comparing the final plan with others made by Arbegast for Osmundson & Staley (and in particular, those images of previously presented Kaiser garden plans), it is clear that the chosen plan was not in Arbegast's usual style, perhaps explaining why he didn't like it. The chosen design bears a resemblance to some of the work of Thomas Church and Brazilian landscape architect Roberto Burle Marx, having no straight lines other than the enclosing walls of the roof. Walks, a reflecting pool, and planting areas comprise a series of undulating curves and meshing biomorphic shapes.

Once the plan was accepted, Arbegast's role was largely finished, and Osmundson had only to complete his share of the actual work by overseeing the installation of the landscape at the ground-level portions of the property, in addition to his usual liaison duties. The roof garden installation was the sole responsibility of John Staley. Kaiser made one proviso: the garden must display the use of Kaiser-made products to the greatest extent possible. Landscape architect John Sue was hired early in 1959 to execute working plans for lighting, planting, grading, and irrigation. Sue also designed custom-made concrete drinking fountains, benches, raised planting beds, and walkways made with Kaiser cement, the bench tops and walkways being finished with exposed aggregate. Light fixtures and electrical wiring featured Kaiser aluminum.[5]

Staley's largest challenges were weight and drainage. Wet soil and trees are heavy items. It was

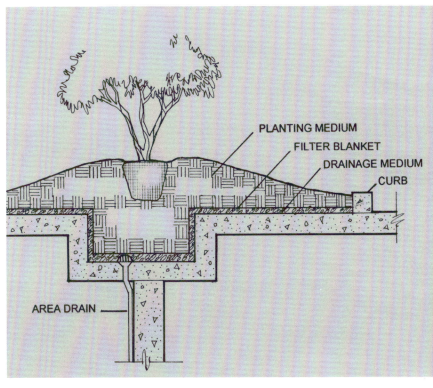

determined that the weight between the garage's supporting columns was limited to 135 pounds per square foot dead load and 15,000 pounds directly over the columns. These figures became ruling factors in every plan for planting the garden. It meant that the heaviest items, the trees, could only be placed over the columns, in a grid pattern. It turned out that Arbegast's design brilliantly (albeit accidentally) disguised this grid so that it is scarcely noticeable, even from an aerial vantage point—unless one knows to look for it. The trees were left in their planting boxes with braces attached to the bases to reduce wind damage; some were placed in large, circular, raised concrete planters, while others had soil mounded around them to disguise the boxes. It was Sue's idea to add a few more random mounds and adjust the grading so that the tree mounds were not so conspicuous, and this enhanced the effect of what Philip Pregill and Nancy Volkman describe in *Landscape in History: Design and Planning in the Eastern and Western Traditions* as a three-dimensional manipulation of the ground plane that created fluid linkages between spaces.[6]

Since none of the present-day technology that makes roof gardens feasible was available in 1959, Staley and his assistants were forced to make it up as they went along. The pioneering use of lightweight soil mix, the choice of a thick layer of straw as a substitute for filter fabric to aid in keeping the soil from washing away before it could stabilize, and topping that with a four-inch layer of lightweight aggregate rock to improve drainage, as well as the choice of plant specimens with fibrous root systems, ensured the Kaiser garden would continue to function relatively well over the next fifty years. Sue was assigned to choose plants having naturally spreading and fibrous roots that would best survive in the relatively shallow soil. The use of lightweight rubber-tired vehicles and dollies on the roof for moving the soil and positioning the heavy, boxed trees was also considered innovative for the time.

The garden was completed in October 1960. Due to severe cost overruns, some changes were made to the original plan during construction. The bridge spanning the pool, a garden shelter meant to provide a focal point, and a windscreen for the north wall were abandoned. The landscaping for the tower roof was

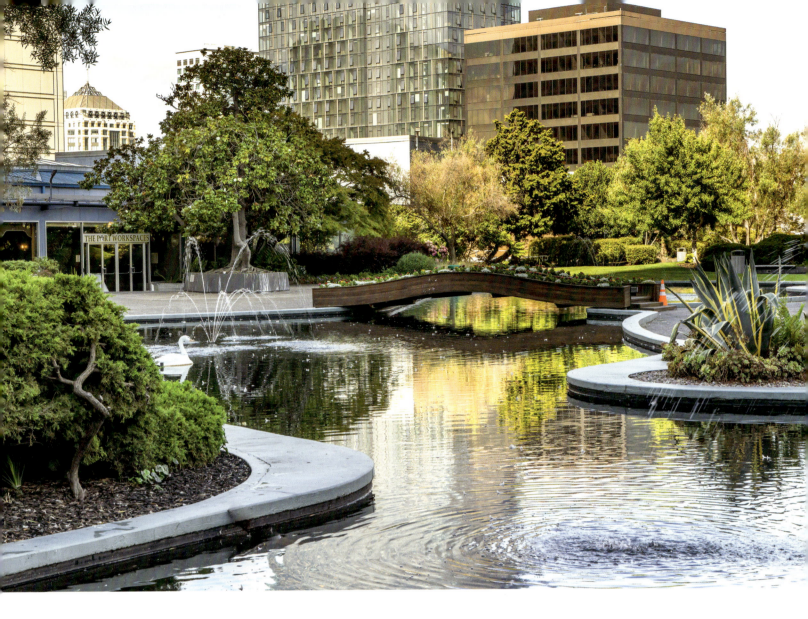

also dropped as impractical due to extreme wind. Mrs. Edgar Kaiser wanted more color in the garden and donated some seven hundred hybrid tea roses to that end.

Gardens are, by nature, ephemeral, and threats to the integrity of this garden followed, beginning as early as 1965, some averted, others not. From the very beginning, drainage proved somewhat faulty, and the roof was always leaking. Proposals to build on top of the garden have largely failed. A garden storage shed was added, as was an inappropriately styled wooden bridge over the reflecting pool. The garden's aluminum night-lighting system failed, and replacement costs were prohibitive. Irrigation systems were replaced due to inefficiency. The greatest physical damage resulted from the 1989 Loma Prieta earthquake. Paving torn up to facilitate repairs to the garage was replaced using materials that did not match the

Above: Later additions to the roof garden included a wooden bridge across the reflecting pool. Opposite: Small elements such as water fountains echo the white simplicity of lines in their Modernist design.

originals in color or texture. Three decorative plant pots disappeared, as did three concrete benches. Those that remain show signs of spalling on the edges. The landscape has suffered as well. Some plants and trees were knocked down by winter storms; others died from too much or too little water and were replaced by less thirsty varieties.[7]

The Kaiser Center was first sold in 2003. Subsequent owners wanted to develop the building's "air rights" by constructing new towers on the property. Summit Commercial Properties, a Southern California firm, terminated the in-house gardeners and hired contractors, then sold the building to San Francisco–based Swig Company in 2005. Swig, too, wanted to eliminate the garden. In 2020, they sold to TMG Partners, which entered into a long-term lease including a purchase option with Pacific Gas and Electric Company to relocate the utility's headquarters from San Francisco. It remains to be seen whether the new owners or their tenants will take responsibility for maintaining the integrity of this iconic garden. In the meantime, the garden is now generating income as a wedding venue, possibly prolonging its preservation.

## PART 3

# EVERYDAY PLACES
## VERNACULAR LANDSCAPES

Cultural geographer J.B. Jackson pioneered the study of vernacular landscapes, or everyday places. He described them as a human-made system of spaces overlaid on the land, where the evolving landscape's function is to serve its community and accommodate cultural change. This chapter looks at vernacular landscapes in three regions from Sonoma in the north, to Monterey on the Central Coast, and San Diego in the south. In each of these regions, the landscapes evolved through use by the people whose occupancy and activities shaped them.

How people manage the land in California reflects their values and resources at a given point in time. Prior to Spanish colonization, what is now California was occupied by an estimated 310,000 Indigenous peoples. There was an abundance of wildlife, streams were full of fish, and shellfish were plentiful along the beaches bordering the Pacific Ocean. Untold thousands of sea otters and whales swam offshore. Sonoma County's landscape history serves as a microcosm for California's landscape transformation. The sequence, progressing from the environment, not a wilderness, which Indigenous communities managed for their benefit, to the Spanish colonial missions and Mexican ranching eras, to full exploitation of the landscape by Americans, is typical for virtually every county in the state.

Founded in 1770, just a year after Spanish colonization began, Monterey served as the Spanish and then the Mexican capital of Alta California until 1848. Attracted by glowing, written descriptions of the city long before California became part of the United States, Americans moved in and brought their vernacular building and garden traditions with them. Familiar plants, such as fruit trees, began to be introduced. However, water limitations imposed by the winter-wet, summer-dry climate still meant there were no lawns, and as in colonial times, things were primarily grown for practical reasons, not as ornamentals. Thomas Larkin, a businessman and politician from Massachusetts, is credited with introducing a new building style in 1835, now called Monterey Colonial, in which the first floor of the house was Mexican-style adobe with a second floor encircled by an American-style balcony. There was a veranda on the ground floor opening to an enclosed, rudimentary garden space.

In the latter part of the nineteenth century, a desire for Spanish-influenced houses and gardens arose throughout California. It was sparked, in part, by Helen Hunt Jackson's 1884 novel *Ramona*, with its romanticized descriptions of lush Mexican-era gardens and kindly mission "padres." However, the gardens of the Mexican Americans she encountered as she wrote the book were already transformed by more abundant water resources that made growing flowers easier. Jackson wrote the novel to

> *"The soil seems well adapted to horticulture, and the climate produces a perpetual spring."*
>
> —Captain George Vancouver upon seeing Monterey, about 1792

appeal to public opinion, in the hope of improving the treatment of the Indigenous population residing in what was by then an American state. The mythology of the flower-filled mission gardens became so widespread that actual gardens soon resembled the myths, and were passed off as authentic to tourists and residents alike. Monterey's old gardens, from the 1920s on, owe more to that mythology and the influence of the Spanish Colonial Revival style of architecture than to the hardscrabble reality of the Indigenous peoples, early colonizers, and American settlers who did not have copious amounts of water to waste on flowers. That changed with American water projects. Perhaps ironically, these pretty, romanticized gardens are now historic themselves. Many are part of Monterey's Old Town Historic District, a National Historic Landmark.

California's Indigenous communities and immigrants of color were fundamental to the development of California's vernacular landscapes. Mexican citizens, whose rancho culture had wrought so many changes on territories taken from Indigenous communities, were discriminated against, and in many cases robbed of *their* land, as Americans took over following the gold rush. Indigenous people were forced onto reservations shortly after California became a state in 1850. This, and the growth of the state's population, resulted in a lack of low-wage laborers. Chinese men immigrated in great numbers to fill the demand for labor. Racial discrimination against the Chinese resulted in an 1882 act prohibiting any future immigration. Another labor shortage ensued, so workers, including people from Japan, immigrated to fill the new demand.

The popularity of Japanese-style gardens in America was the result of their construction during exhibitions and world fairs. Japanese immigrants and their American-born children had an impact on the landscape as they moved from being simple laborers into garden maintenance, garden design, and farming. The lives of Japanese American gardeners and farmers were upended when almost all of them were interned during World War II. Many did not return to farming and gardening after they gained their freedom, and those roles were often later filled by new immigrants from Mexico. Ongoing cultural changes in California mean that vernacular landscapes continue to evolve.

Overleaf: Perkins Park, extending along the bluffs in Pacific Grove in Monterey County, is a vernacular landscape developed over many years, first by Hayes Perkins beginning in 1943 using carpets of pink *Drosanthemum floribundum*, torch aloe (*Aloe arborescens*), and other succulents, and later by the city and native plant enthusiasts.

# SONOMA COUNTY'S LANDSCAPE HISTORY

Thomas A. Brown

## THE SPANISH SETTLEMENT PERIOD

Sonoma was the first permanent town in the future Sonoma County, and the place where the California Republic was founded in 1846. Its name is believed to derive from an Indigenous word, as the land in what is now Sonoma County was initially home to the Pomo, Wappo, and Coast Miwok communities, among others. They did not practice agriculture—cultivating livestock and growing groups of plants systematically for food or livestock forage. Instead, they relied on local plants for food and to supply many practical needs. Wild animals, shellfish, and salmon provided most of their protein. Their impact on the land was significant through the management tactic of prescribed burning, which cleared the land around oak trees to make it easier to hunt and gather acorns, one of their dietary staples. Prescribed burns were also utilized to produce the straight shoots of the sedges (*Carex* spp.) and other plants used in their intricate basketry work, a horticultural technique similar to coppicing.[1]

Moving north from its missions in Baja California, Spain began colonizing Alta California in San Diego in 1769. This string of Catholic, Franciscan missions and four military garrisons, called presidios, reached the San Francisco Bay in 1776. Along the way, some Indigenous people were converted to Christianity, and many were forced to live in the missions and pressed into service to perform the herding, farming, and other tasks essential to the colonizing efforts, including

Above: Drawing of Mission San Francisco de Asis (Dolores) by lithographer, Captain William Smyth, done in about 1839. Opposite: Landscape management techniques were practiced by the Indigenous people in California in various ways including promoting the growth of straight plants shoots for basketry and cordage through prescribed burns. Cecilia Joaquin, a Pomo woman as documented by Edward S. Curtis about 1924 in what is today's Sonoma County, is shown gathering seeds into an intricately woven burden basket.

building the missions and their water systems. Late in the eighteenth century, soldiers from the San Francisco Presidio occasionally explored areas in what are now the counties of Marin, Sonoma, and Napa, at that time accessible mainly by boat.

The first farmers in Sonoma County were actually Russians, who built Fort Ross on the Pacific coast in 1812 after colonizing Alaska. The intention was to supply their Alaska fur-trade colonies of Sitka, Kodiak, and Unalaska with food from fields, orchards, and livestock, along with the pelts of sea otters caught by the Alaskan Native Alutiiq (Aleuts) who accompanied them. A German botanist on a Russian scientific expedition gave the California poppy (now the state flower) its botanical name, *Eschscholzia californica*.

## THE MEXICAN ERA

In 1823, Californios learned Mexico had won its independence from Spain, which made Alta California a province of the new nation. To discourage Russians from expanding beyond Fort Ross to the San Francisco Bay Area, the Mexican government created a new settlement close to Fort Ross in the Sonoma Valley in 1824. Here, the priest (or "padre") José Altimira founded Mission San Francisco Solano. This mission would be the last and northernmost in the chain of twenty-one and the only mission established under

Mexican rule. Building construction began in October with the new mission sited about two hundred feet north of an Indigenous village. An open space between the mission and village served as a public square, or plaza. European-style agriculture quickly began with a variety of crops, originally native to the New World, such as potatoes, tomatoes, pumpkin, and peppers, near a small stream that irrigated them. Also planted were trees for fruit and shade and a vineyard for sacramental wine. Three years after its founding, the mission's Indigenous population rebelled against the cruel Altimira. He fled back to Spain, and another priest took his place.

In 1833, to check further Russian expansion, the governor put a young ensign, Mariano Guadalupe

Below: Mexican Comandante Vallejo on horseback, his troops, and "Indian Auxiliaries" on the Sonoma plaza with the Sonoma mission in its original configuration to the far right adjacent to the barracks and Vallejo's Casa Grande, which is depicted with an overly tall tower in this view by artist Oriana Day commissioned by Vallejo c. 1879 when he was an old man. Opposite: Fort Ross on the Sonoma coast was built by Russians from about 1812 to 1841 and reconstructed from ruins to become a State Park in the twentieth century.

Vallejo (1807–1890), in charge of starting two civilian settlements in the valleys where the cities of Santa Rosa and Petaluma are now located. These ventures ended when the Catholic Church insisted that the lands belonged to Mission San Francisco Solano. The following year, the decree that secularized all California missions required the church to give up its land ownership. Vallejo, elevated to the rank of *Comandante*, was ordered to house and command a garrison of troops near the mission. He also was to dispose of the mission's temporal assets. Intelligent, resourceful, and energetic, he and his relatives were well positioned to benefit from secularization. Using the labor of Indigenous people at the mission, Vallejo relocated the mission's vineyards to his vast ranch and eventually became famous for his wine. To the west of the mission, he laid out a large plaza. On its north side, he built a barracks for the garrison and, next to it, the two-story Casa Grande with his office on the ground floor and his residence above. This would become the pueblo, or town, of Sonoma. (When he retired, he built a Gothic Victorian–style house on his estate on the outskirts of town called Lachryma Montis.)

Initially the Franciscan priests at the missions had been tasked with training the Indigenous residents to become productive and self-sufficient Christians, whereupon they were to receive their own land. This rarely happened, and in the chaotic period following secularization, people who had lived and worked at Mission San Francisco Solano became homeless. Vallejo provided hundreds of them with food and a place to stay in exchange for tending his large cattle herds and flocks of sheep, making goods in his workshops, cultivating his vineyards, and building his huge second home on his 66,000-acre Rancho Petaluma, the largest adobe ever constructed in Alta California.[2]

The major occupations in the region in the 1830s and 1840s, as elsewhere in Mexican California, were cattle and sheep ranching on former mission lands. The new rancho-owning Californio families grew crops for themselves and their workers, including the cattle-tending vaqueros—most of them Indigenous or of mixed Indigenous and European ancestry—the original cowboys. During these early years in Alta California, the natural environment declined and was transformed. In valleys and adjacent hillsides, woodlands disappeared as trees were cut down for building material and firewood. Grazing had a huge effect: introduced invasive grass species out-competed the native grasses, many of which were perennial bunchgrasses that had stayed green for much of the year. Cattle trampled plants essential to the Indigenous way of life. Sheep and goats not only ate the bunchgrasses but also pulled up their roots. Feral pigs ate the acorns many Indigenous communities relied on for food. Immigrants, mostly Americans, increasingly were arriving. Eager to occupy the land, they set up enterprises that required particular skills lacking among the Californios in their rancho-focused economy. By 1841, the Russians had abandoned Fort Ross because the local sea otter population had been exterminated and farming yields were disappointing.

## THE AMERICAN PERIOD

The first great challenge to Mexican rule in California erupted in Sonoma in 1846. Several dozen armed Americans stormed the plaza on June 14, took General Vallejo captive, and raised their handmade grizzly bear flag. However, the United States had already declared war against Mexico. By February 1848, the war had officially ended and the transition from territory to US statehood began. Shortly after the Mexican War ended, gold was discovered in the Sierra Nevada foothills, resulting in thousands of people migrating to California. It is often said that the gold rush that began in 1849 created more fortunes among those who supplied

the miners than among the miners themselves. People needed to eat, so it was urgent to produce food in areas close to San Francisco, the entry point for aspiring miners and the transshipment center for goods of all kinds traveling up and down the Sacramento River. Sonoma area farmers quickly responded, and the population began to boom. Even before the American takeover, settlers in California had made some changes in the appearance of both its natural and rancho-altered landscapes by introducing machinery invented and widely used elsewhere. By the 1840s, the lumbering industry had begun. Coming from a culture and tradition of forestland, Americans and northern European immigrants consumed far more wood than the Mexicans had in building their homes and outbuildings of adobe bricks. In the 1850s, lumbering extended

Above: Vallejo's Petaluma adobe home was built by Indigenous laborers on his forty-four-thousand-acre ranch. Below Left: Luther Burbank's portrait was reproduced in numerous books and articles. Below Right: 'Santa Rosa' plums in a nineteenth-century bowl typical of the ceramics imported from China for Chinese workers and derogatively known as "Coolie Ware." Overleaf: Vineyards, tasting rooms, and development dominate the Sonoma County landscape today.

into the valleys of the Russian River with their dense stands of redwood trees.

Farmers benefited as more cleared lands became available for crops, orchards, and livestock, as well as sites for new settlements. Petaluma had an early advantage shipping goods and farm products due to its navigable river, called Petaluma Creek, and the town soon became the shipping hub for cargoes of potatoes, fruit, grain, dairy products, eggs, and hay for horse feed. New residents in Sonoma needed orchard and shade trees, plants, and the skilled people who would import, reproduce, and prepare them for sale—both nursery workers and knowledgeable horticulturists. By the late nineteenth century, Sonoma County's agricultural output was best known for fruits, especially apples and plums. The need to propagate fruit-tree rootstock and scions for grafting called for specialized nurseries and experienced grafters.

Petaluma, with its river as the main entry into the interior, kept growing as the county's commercial hub. In the 1860s, the river was improved when a deeper channel was dredged. This provided access for larger boats and small paddle-wheel steamers. Chinese laborers, who had replaced Indigenous laborers forced onto reservations, were hired to do the river improvements. They also tended vineyards, crushed grapes, dug wine caves, and would later work on the railroads.

## SANTA ROSA'S PREEMINENCE IN HORTICULTURE

During the almost eighty years of Spanish and Mexican control of California, about 250 species of plants were introduced. By comparison, during the next half century—up to 1900—over 11,000 species and varieties of fruit, cereals, forage, ornamental plants, and inevitably, weeds, were introduced into California. It would be largely nurserymen and women, a new and expanding profession in California, who arranged for this flood of plants to satisfy the demands of the many new residents and wealthy estate owners who wanted novel things for their extensive gardens and conservatories.

The first nurserymen in California knew little about the peculiarities of its climate. They introduced species familiar to them from colder places. It took a few years to realize that plants that needed to be carefully protected in greenhouses during eastern winters were perfectly hardy out-of-doors in this far western state. Nurseries then began importing many broad-leaved evergreen species from other Mediterranean-climate regions of the world, such as in Italy, Australia, and South Africa.

By the turn of the nineteenth century, Santa Rosa's preeminence in horticulture within Sonoma County and throughout the world was secured because it was the home of the so-called "Plant Wizard" from Massachusetts, Luther Burbank. In addition to his own plant breeding projects, Burbank accepted commissions from other nurseries and seed houses to transform existing plants by increasing flower size, creating new colors, introducing disease resistance, improving the flavor of edibles, or encouraging the development of other traits held to be desirable. Inspired by Charles Darwin, his method of hybridization essentially sped up natural selection and resulted in about eight hundred new varieties, including the plumcot, the ancestor of the Idaho potato, and a spineless beaver-tail *Opuntia* cactus. His fame would rest secure on the creation of just two plants—the Shasta daisy and the 'Santa Rosa' plum. Burbank also operated Gold Ridge Experiment Farm in Sebastopol, eight miles west of Santa Rosa, where he is buried. Impressed by his achievements, shortly after he died, the artist Frida Kahlo painted a Surrealistic portrait of Burbank, depicting him as a hybrid half man, half tree. Aside from Burbank, nurserymen and women seldom pop up in the official history of the state, yet these people played a large role in changing the face of California. Their work literally lives on. Perhaps one measure of their success can be seen in the fact that, apart from native plants in natural areas, something like 90 percent of the plants we see are introduced species.

By 1935, Sonoma County was ranked tenth in agricultural production among all the nation's counties. Things began to change after World War II. Petaluma's once-ubiquitous chicken ranches have disappeared. The orchards and ranches that dominated the cultivated landscape have now mostly given way to vineyards, tasting rooms, and houses.

Despite the success of Pomona, or agriculture, in Sonoma County, Bacchus, the god of wine, triumphed. The wine grape is the most economically significant crop for the region. The county has also become a haven for organic farmers, who produce specialty crops and cheeses that are featured at upscale restaurants along with its excellent wines. The range of microclimates and various soil types, coupled with a relative sufficiency of good-quality water and the pressure to develop, suggest that the story of both agriculture and horticulture in Sonoma County has many chapters yet to be written.

Luther Burbank's spineless *Opuntia* cactus in the contemporary display garden behind Burbank's Gold Ridge Experimental Farm cottage.

# HISTORIC GARDENS OF OLD MONTEREY

David A. Laws

One of the oldest European settlements on the West Coast, Monterey, founded in 1770, served as the original Spanish and later the Mexican capital of California. The city also played an important role in the early political development of the modern American state when, in 1849, delegates to the convention that drafted California's first constitution met in Colton Hall, now preserved as a museum that displays original artifacts and documents from that meeting.

Since the late eighteenth century, historical figures visiting the area have commented on the natural beauty of the setting. When he was anchored in the Monterey harbor in the late eighteenth century, Captain George Vancouver wrote, "The climate produces a perpetual spring." In *A Voyage to California, the Sandwich Islands, and Around the World*, French sea captain August Duhaut-Cilly observed in the early nineteenth century that the hills were "carpeted with green grass and shaded by great conifers and fine oaks. These trees are sometimes grouped so attractively that they may have been planted by a skilled designer." American sailor Richard Henry Dana wrote in *Two Years Before the Mast* (1840) that "Monterey, as far as my observation goes, is decidedly the pleasantest and most civilized-looking place in California.… The soil is rich as man could wish, climate as good as any in the world, water abundant and situation extremely beautiful."

The Monterey Peninsula is home to many buildings dating from those times. The City of Monterey Community Development Department claims that in addition to early American-era buildings, "Monterey has preserved more original Mexican-era adobes than any other city in California." In 1970, the National Park Service (NPS) declared Monterey's Old Town Historic District a National Historic Landmark. Today, the NPS interprets this landmark district in the context of "American Latino Heritage."

The gardens surrounding the Carmel Mission are relatively recent and typical of the "romantic twaddle" that has been represented as authentic to the Spanish Colonial era of the 1770s.

Garden historian Judith Taylor explains in *Tangible Memories: Californians and their Gardens* why, with such a wealth of venerable architecture in a spectacular, ocean-front setting, the Monterey Peninsula has few gardens that represent the horticulture of those times.

"Garden lovers will find little distinctly Spanish in the Monterey gardens of today and very little that is early American....This is hardly surprising. [There were] very few resources for creating gardens, and water was always very scarce in the summers. If the civic groups in charge of restoring Monterey to its original condition had adhered to strict authenticity, the town would seem very dreary now."

Many of today's "period" gardens were installed on sites where only fragments of the original hardscape and horticultural materials remained. However, as Frances Grate noted in an article for the California Garden & Landscape Society's annual conference, held in Monterey in 2000, "Although the gardens have all evolved largely during this century, each is an integral part of the house it surrounds." The late landscape architect and historian Thomas A. Brown, who presented "The Landscape and Development of Early Monterey" at the meeting, was less charitable. He described what the "gardens really were like as opposed to the romantic twaddle palmed off on unsuspecting tourists." As with the fountain and rose-filled courtyards of today's Carmel Mission (Mission San Carlos Borromeo del Rio Carmelo), most modern "period" gardens owe more to Victorian visions of fictional characters like Ramona and Zorro than to the hardscrabble lives of the Spanish colonizers, pioneering settlers, and Indigenous laborers.

Whether truly "historic," romanticized "twaddle," or something else again, the following gardens have provided inspiration and pleasure for generations of Monterey Peninsula artists, residents, and visitors. Many are now historic themselves as examples of Pe-

riod Revival and Colonial Revival–style gardens. Unless otherwise noted, the gardens are associated with buildings of the Monterey State Historic Park and are within the National Historic Landmark district. All are located along the "Path of History," a self-guided walking tour identified by round yellow tile markers set in the sidewalks of downtown.

## PACIFIC HOUSE

Built in 1847 by Thomas Oliver Larkin, the first (and only) US Consul to Mexican California, the two-story adobe known as Pacific House on the Custom House Plaza has served as a tavern, a hotel, county offices, a church, and a ballroom, among other things. Today it houses a museum that tells the story of Monterey as the capital of Spanish California. In *Sketches of Leading Places of Interest in Monterey County*, Hattie Morley wrote in 1896 that the "backyard, which is surrounded by a high adobe wall, was a place of great excitement and interest. Great bear and bullfights took place there." Margaret Jacks, who owned the building in the 1920s, contracted with the Olmsted Brothers landscape architecture firm to transform the bare ground into a romanticized, Spanish Colonial Revival–style courtyard for more peaceful gatherings. Plans for the Spanish-style walled garden, extensive correspondence, and a planting list are held at the Frederick Law Olmsted National Historic Site in Brookline, Massachusetts.

The garden, known as the Memory Garden, is enclosed by Pacific House on the east and high adobe walls on the other three sides. Four southern magnolia trees shade a bronze figure in a central fountain. Tile-

topped, arched verandas and wooden pergolas support Chinese wisteria vines, climbing roses, and an ancient, twisted-trunk tea tree (*Leptospermum laevigatum*). The northern section, separated by an arched adobe wall, was meant to serve as a tea garden. The west wall features an outdoor kitchen. In 1939–1940, a large grill was installed in the center because of the great popularity of the annual Merienda festival commemorating the founding of Monterey in 1770. The garden is the most visited in Monterey State Historic Park and is a popular venue for weddings and celebrations. In the western wall, a heavy wooden door opens to the Sensory Garden with a multi-tiered fountain, bougainvillea, and colorful hanging baskets lining a brick-paved pedestrian section of Olivier Street and the Casa del Oro adobe, where miners returning from the gold fields in the 1850s are said to have stored their booty.

## OLD WHALING STATION ADOBE

Purple wisteria vines trail over high stone walls and an overhanging balcony at the two-story Old Whaling Station Adobe and Garden. A small brick-lined garden and patio now provide a setting for special events.

Scottish immigrant David Wright built the house for his family in 1847. A front sidewalk of whale vertebrae cut into diamond patterns for paving recalls its later service as a whale oil rendering operation before commercial whaling in the Pacific Ocean led to the near extinction of gray whales.

## CALIFORNIA'S FIRST THEATRE

English sailor Jack Swann constructed this adobe as a saloon and lodgings circa 1844. It became California's First Theatre in 1848 when a group of soldiers from Colonel Stevenson's regiment of New Yorkers staged plays and comedies.

The current garden, behind a wooden fence at Pacific and Scott Streets, was laid out in the 1920s in the shadow of two giant Monterey cypress trees (*Hesperocyparis*, formerly *Cupressus macrocarpa*). The cypress trees have been removed, but the original stone-edged, gravel paths still meander between borders of colorful bedding plants, succulents, and ferns. A handsome cup-of-gold vine (*Solandra maxima*) is espaliered against the south-facing adobe wall.

## CASA SOBERANES

Casa Soberanes, known as the "House of the Blue Gate," is a two-story adobe with a cantilevered balcony dating from 1842. Ezequiel Soberanes Jr., a gardener at the Carmel Mission who inherited the property from his father, began developing the garden around the turn of the last century. Photographs from 1905 show a thriving front yard. In the 1920s, his successors, Ruben and Jean Serrano, built the stone retaining wall around the boundary and laid out walks and beds edged with abalone shells, upended crocks, and wine bottles. Plantings consist of an eclectic selection of colorful material acquired over the years. Victorian-style boxwood hedges line beds filled with lavender, rosemary, daylily, hebe, geranium, gazania, and old roses.

## VÁSQUEZ ADOBE

The city-owned Vásquez Adobe at 546 Dutra Street, the family home of infamous outlaw Tiburcio Vásquez, presents a disappointing appearance compared to a circa 1935 painting by WPA artist Evelyn McCormick. Her rendering includes the

Above: A cup-of-gold vine (*Solandra maxima*) is espaliered against a wall of California's First Theatre. Below: This painting by WPA artist M. Evelyn McCormick of the 1830s Vásquez Adobe in Monterey shows it with 1920s-era romanticized plantings and an added second story. Opposite: Bullfights took place in this space behind the Pacific House before it was redesigned by the Olmsted Brothers and named The Memory Garden.

Old Larkin Home
Monterey, Calif.
zſ 394

added second story, climbing roses, and massed pots of colorful geraniums. Today's landscaping is most notable for the original bronze statue of Dennis the Menace that was stolen from a children's park in 2006, recovered ten years later, and relocated here.

## LARKIN HOUSE

Thomas Larkin built his two-story, white-washed home, Larkin House, in 1835 and walled the garden as early as 1842. He combined timber framing traditions from his native New England with local adobe to construct one of the first two-story houses in California. The double verandas evoke Larkin's time in South Carolina and have become a defining characteristic of the still-popular Monterey Colonial style of architecture. Elvira Abrego, a grandniece of General Mariano Vallejo (who helped guide the transition of Alta California from a territory of Mexico to the US state of California), wrote in 1896 that "a large orchard containing many varieties of fruit trees originally surrounded the house and a few of them are still standing."

Larkin's granddaughter, Alice Larkin Toulmin, developed the existing garden during the 1920s and 1930s. Its features include the Sherman Quarters, an

1834 single-room stone structure occupied in 1847 by the future Union General William Tecumseh Sherman during the US occupation of Mexican California. A water-storage cistern covered with an ornate wrought iron grate and high, tile-topped walls that provide seclusion from the bustling city beyond are other garden features. Mature trees, flowering shrubs, and an arbor covered with a 'Climbing Cécile Brünner' rose shade raised beds packed with perennials.

## CASA AMESTI

Between 1833 and 1855, Jose Amesti built a house and enclosed his property with a twelve-foot-tall adobe wall at 516 Polk Street. Interior designer Frances Adler Elkins purchased the structure in 1919 and rehabilitated the adobe as a home and showplace for her business. Her brother, Chicago architect David Adler, designed the formal garden with gravel paths and boxwood hedges inspired by a courtyard they visited at the Alhambra in Granada, Spain. Elkins lived at Casa Amesti until she died in 1953. The property is now owned by a private club.

## COOPER MOLERA ADOBE

American sea captain John Rogers Cooper arrived in Monterey in 1823. In order to own property, he married Incarnación Vallejo (General Mariano Vallejo's sister) and became a Mexican citizen, then built their adobe home in 1827. Over many years and ownership changes, his walled, two-acre holding expanded to include two adobe houses, barns, a cookhouse, and a warehouse. Now called the Cooper Molera Adobe, it is

Above: The Larkin House garden, designed by Larkin's granddaughter, had romantic lush plantings, vines climbing to the balconies, and a palm tree. The cottage to the left in the garden is known as the "Sherman Quarters." Opposite: Known as the House of the Blue Gate, Casa Soberanes has 1920s-era garden beds edged with abalone shells and upended wine bottles.

a National Historic Landmark and National Trust Historic Site repurposed into a museum, restaurant, retail, and event complex with English-style flower gardens.

Horticulture books on growing stone fruits were found in the Cooper library, and family accounts record shipments of cherry trees as early as 1846. On-site archeological investigations uncovered peach pits. All are indications that the Coopers cultivated a small orchard in their walled compound. An interpretive plaque in the modern orchard, titled Teaching Garden (1832–1900), lists almond, fig, pear, walnut, and apple varieties that would have been available in Cooper's time.

'Chromatella' (or 'Cloth of Gold'), a climbing Noisette rose, grows against the orchard wall. Known locally as the "Sherman rose," this pale-yellow bloom is associated with a popular legend of the late 1800s concerning William T. Sherman's military service in Monterey. The legend tells that the young lieutenant presented a cutting of the rose to the beautiful senorita Maria Ignatia Bonifacio and promised to return to wed her by the time it took root and bloomed. Instead, in 1850 he married the daughter of a prominent politician in Washington and never returned to Monterey.

According to rosarians, the first cuttings of the rose did not arrive in Monterey until twenty-five years after Sherman left in 1847, but fueled by an energetic promoter, the fable drove a boom in yellow roses

*Above Right: Maria Bonifacio's home, Casa Bonifacio, with a 'Chromatella' rose (above left) on the arbor over the gate was painted by M. Evelyn McCormick in about 1935 before the adobe house was moved to avoid demolition. Opposite: Both the Cooper Molera Adobe and its gardens are considered vernacular, as they were developed and altered over many years. This garden has been remodeled.*

and quaint tea rooms. Featured in postcards, senorita Bonifacio's black-clothed presence and rose-covered arbor outside her adobe home on Alvarado Street was a tourist landmark as was the "Sherman Rose Tea Room" at the house. To avoid demolition, in 1922 artist Percy Gray moved the Casa Bonifacio adobe and the rose to a new site at 785 Mesa Road, where it is called the Sherman Rose Cottage (often confused with the Sherman Quarters at the Larkin House).

## ROBERT LOUIS STEVENSON HOUSE

Robert Louis Stevenson, the Scottish author of *Treasure Island*, lodged at the French Hotel on Houston Street in 1879 while pursuing his future wife, Fanny Osbourne, who was staying at Casa Bonifacio. In his 1913 travelogue, *California Coast Trails*, English horseback traveler J. Smeaton Chase described the rear yard as "a square of garden ground, in a corner of which a few nasturtiums and stalks of mint grew in a secret and furtive manner." The house is now a museum showcasing an extensive collection of Stevenson memorabilia. The garden that covers about half an acre is in a romantic cottage style with winding paths and densely planted beds of annuals, perenniáls, and shrubs. Notable trees include figs and southern magnolia. The layout and trees largely date from the early twentieth century, before the property was donated to the state. The garden was renewed by state parks staff in 1948 and again in the 1980s.

## THE HOTEL DEL MONTE ARIZONA GARDEN

Monterey's oldest garden to retain much of its original design and appropriate plantings lies east of downtown on the former Hotel del Monte grounds. This property, now the campus of the Naval Postgraduate School, is accessible only by military personnel or their guests.

German-born landscape architect Rudolf Ulrich created the first of his signature "Arizona gardens" as part of his elaborate plan for the 127 acres of the Hotel del Monte, which opened in 1880 and was rebuilt twice following devastating fires. Ulrich's garden featured prominently in Hotel del Monte literature and marketing promotions. He filled fifty-seven raised beds arranged in a symmetrical, geometric design covering over thirty thousand square feet, edged with serpentine rock and filled with succulents and other species collected in Arizona and Mexico's Sonora Desert. According to Julie Cain, an expert on Ulrich's Arizona gardens, "The variety and rarity of the plants and the use of formal design was absolutely unique in California at the time. Guests...were suitably impressed by this seaside desert garden, often posing for photographs amongst the plants."

After years of neglect, in 1993, the US Navy, which acquired the hotel and grounds during World War II, funded seeds and materials for restoration by "Friends of the Arizona Garden" volunteers. In 2010, volunteers launched another restoration effort to re-create as much as possible of the original design as described in an 1888 record of the garden's plant list and landscape.

Public and private organizations play essential roles in preserving Monterey's historic buildings and gardens. The Monterey State Historic Park Association assists California State Parks by raising funds to support interpretation and educational programs and preserve Monterey's landmark buildings and cultural heritage. For over twenty-five years, members of the Historic Garden League have been helping to maintain the area's significant historic gardens. Volunteers lead garden tours, serve on work parties, and perform fundraising activities that benefit everyone who loves Old Monterey.

Painted by WPA artist M. Evelyn McCormick before its demise and later restoration, the "Arizona Garden" at the Hotel del Monte was created by Rudolf Ulrich in the late nineteenth century. Opposite: Although she denied a romance with William T. Sherman, Maria Bonifacio posed for postcards and had a tea room, one of several with yellow roses that cashed in on the legend.

The US Census for California tallied fewer than 100 people of Japanese ancestry residing in the state in 1880, although there were many Chinese residents. Widespread racial discrimination led to the passage in 1882 of the Chinese Exclusion Act, prohibiting immigration from China. The result was a labor shortage, so workers from the eastern United States and other countries, including Japan, came to California to fill low-wage jobs in the booming economy. Water for the fledgling city of San Diego and its farmlands was provided by two new dams, and by 1887, San Diego was a boomtown, attracting winter and permanent residents.

Japanese-style gardens became popular in the United States in the 1880s. Edward S. Morse's book *Japanese Homes and Their Surroundings* and Josiah Conder's *Landscape Gardening in Japan* spread the trend. The Japanese government used international expositions to disseminate knowledge about Japanese culture to the West. Japanese gardens were featured at Philadelphia's 1876 Centennial Exposition and Chicago's 1893 World's Columbian Exposition. At the 1894 California Midwinter International Exposition in San Francisco's Golden Gate Park, Asian art importer George Turner Marsh, who had lived in Japan, was

Below: This postcard of the Japanese Tea Garden at the Hotel del Coronado depicts a lady wearing a kimono who was probably a waitress in the teahouse. Opposite: The Japanese Tea Garden in San Francisco's Golden Gate Park dates from 1894 and launched a vogue for commercial tea gardens.

4314. Japanese Tea Garden, Coronado, San Diego, Cal.

4423. Japanese Tea House, Panama-California Exposition, San Diego, 1915.

granted the concession for a Japanese village and tea garden. His tea garden was a grand success. Japanese women dressed in kimonos served tea and rice cakes in a teahouse constructed by Japanese craftsmen. Japanese gardeners tended the traditional tea garden. The village was dismantled after the expo, but the tea garden and teahouse remained, operated and cared for by the Hagiwara family. According to historian Kendall Brown, it "launched a vogue for commercial tea gardens."[1]

Quick to realize the benefits of such a tourist attraction, sugar magnate John Spreckels envisioned a Japanese teahouse near his Hotel del Coronado in San Diego. In 1902, he convinced George Turner Marsh to build a tea garden on land along the beach in Coronado.

Marsh later built several more Japanese-style gardens in various cities, some of them in conjunction with hotel shops where Japanese stone lanterns and artifacts were offered for sale. The famous Japanese Garden on Henry Huntington's estate in San Marino began when Marsh's Pasadena tea garden failed. In 1912, Marsh sold the teahouse, mature plants, and ornaments to Huntington, who soon added other features, including the full moon bridge constructed by Japanese craftsmen.

Marsh's Coronado concession thrived, however. Japanese men demeaningly dressed as coolies pulled rickshaws to take hotel guests up Ocean Boulevard to the tea garden tended by Japanese gardeners. Golfers were able to quench their thirst after finishing a round at the course adjacent to the teahouse. The tea garden was destroyed in 1905 by a huge storm and ocean surge. Marsh built a new, improved tea garden on higher ground near the hotel. It closed in 1939 when the hotel was sold.

Japanese immigrants (*Issei*) were not just gardeners and teahouse waitresses; many had landscape maintenance businesses or went into farming. There were thirty-two Japanese-owned or leased farms in Mission Valley and in the South Bay area of San Diego County by 1905. More were later established in the county, including the Chino family farm. Japanese farmers introduced bell peppers, strawberries,

For the 1915 Panama-California Exposition in Balboa Park a pavilion modeled on a Kyoto temple served as the teahouse.

asparagus, and winter celery to the region and were noted for their flowers, potatoes, cantaloupes, cucumbers, and tomatoes.

San Diego's Chamber of Commerce formed an exposition committee in 1909 dedicated to hosting an exposition in 1915 to celebrate the opening of the Panama Canal. Despite financial backing by Spreckels and others, in the end the role of host city for the Panama-Pacific International Exposition was awarded to San Francisco. Undaunted, San Diego decided to go ahead with its own, smaller version: the Panama-California Exposition in Balboa Park.

The proposed opening of the Japanese tea garden at the San Francisco Exposition stirred up a hornet's nest that touched on the social dichotomy then existing in California: Japanese gardens were well liked; Japanese immigrants were not, at least not by certain influential politicians, labor leaders, and the conservative press. The tea garden became the focus of political posturing. The California legislature was preparing to pass the Alien Land Law, legislation that would prevent Japanese immigrants from owning agricultural land or leasing it for more than three years. In protest against this policy change, the Japanese government canceled their participation in the San Francisco Exposition. Local businessmen who did not want the Japanese government to withdraw their economic support for the tea garden tried to get the vote on the measure postponed until after the expo. California Senator James D. Phelan, former San Francisco mayor and founder of the Japanese Exclusion League, said, "Japan may not choose to exhibit at our fair, but we cannot sell our birthright for a tea garden.' An editorial in the *Sacramento-Union* stated, "We believe labor

desires the Japanese burden off its shoulders…and that it will not be lured from its opposition by the promise of the most beautiful tea-garden that the mind of Oriental man has conceived." In the end, the Alien Land Law passed in 1913, and Japan participated in the 1915 San Francisco Expo.

Despite the prejudice against Japanese people displayed in San Francisco, the tea garden at the 1915 San Diego Expo was popular. Watanabe & Shibada Trade Association created a Japanese-style garden and teahouse called the Tea Pavilion. It was designed by K. Tamai and modeled after an elaborate temple

Above: Before they were sent to the incarceration camps, people were processed at the Santa Anita Racetrack and housed in the horse stables. Below: This miniature Japanese-style landscape expressed the creativity of people incarcerated at the Poston, Arizona concentration camp during World War II. Opposite: The Ono Family Produce market in San Diego where some of the many things introduced to the area by Japanese American farmers were sold.

in Kyoto, not a simple teahouse. Parts made in Japan were assembled in San Diego by Japanese carpenters. One-hundred-year-old pines barely three feet tall were imported from Japan for the garden along with stone lanterns and bronze cranes. Japanese women dressed in kimonos served visitors tea and rice cakes inside the Tea Pavilion and on the veranda. At the close of the exposition, Hachisaku Asakawa and his wife, Osamu, leased the Tea Pavilion from the city. Hachisaku farmed in Mission Valley, while Osamu operated the tea garden concession up until the start of World War II.

In the early decades of the twentieth century, most Japanese gardeners and farmers in California had been successful at adapting to their new homeland despite racial prejudice such as the Alien Land Law of 1913, the 1922 Supreme Court ruling that Japanese immigrants were not eligible to become citizens, and the Immigration Act of 1924, outlawing further immigration from Japan. With the onset of World War II, the lives of these and other Japanese Americans took a decided turn for the worse. The surprise December 1941 attack on Pearl Harbor in Hawaii raised fears of similar Japanese attacks aided by Japanese residents in cities along the West Coast. In February 1942, President Franklin D. Roosevelt issued Executive Order 9066, which led to the three-year imprisonment of nearly 120,000 people of Japanese ancestry living in southern Arizona and the coastal states of Washington, Oregon, and California, even though the majority were American citizens by right of birth.

The Hagiwara family (proprietors of the Golden Gate Park Tea Garden), the Asakawa family (operators

Above: Ben Segawa returned to San Diego from Poston, where he was incarcerated as a boy, and had a long career in agriculture. Opposite: Japanese cherry trees in bloom at the Japanese Friendship Garden in San Diego, which was finally completed in 2015.

of the Balboa Park Tea Pavilion), and the Chino family of farmers were interned, along with many other Japanese Americans. The Asakawas were initially sent to the "assembly center" at the Santa Anita Racetrack holding area in Arcadia while the concentration "internment" camps were being built. Their twenty-seven-year-old son, Moto; his wife, Florence; and baby son, Bruce, were also confined there. Moto had earned the rank of Eagle Scout, graduated in 1938 from the University of California at Berkeley, and was a farmer in Mission Valley. From Santa Anita, the extended Asakawa family was sent on to the new incarceration camp in Poston, Arizona, as were most Japanese Americans from San Diego County.

At the age of eleven, Ben Segawa was incarcerated along with his parents and nine brothers and sisters. His family had farmed in San Diego's South Bay. They, too, were first sent to Santa Anita and later moved to Poston. When *Nisei* (second generation) American-born Japanese children were being shipped off to the camps, San Diego Public Library children's librarian Clara Breed went to the train station and gave each of them stamped, self-addressed postcards. "Write to me," she told them, "and I will send you books and other things you might need." Breed saved the postcards and letters she received, and they are featured in the book *Dear Miss Breed* by Joanne Oppenheim.

As the camps were being closed at the end of the war, anti-Japanese feelings were still alive. Many Japanese Americans had fears about returning to communities that had shown such strong prejudice against them. When they were released from the camps, 55 percent of Japanese Americans from San Diego chose to settle elsewhere. Moto Asakawa decided to return to San Diego with his family. Upon arrival he found that the State of California had confiscated his Mission Valley farmland. With his brother George, Moto successfully sued the state and regained the property. In 1950, he opened a retail nursery, the Presidio Garden Center. Asakawa became one of the most-respected nurserymen in the county and served as president of the California Association of Nurseries in the 1970s.

Unlike many third-generation Japanese Americans, Moto Asakawa's son Bruce chose to follow his father into horticulture. He, too, became a respected San Diego nurseryman and operated the Bonita Garden Center until 1985. Bruce Asakawa was a landscape architect and, with his wife, Sharon, authored gardening books, including the well-regarded *California's Garden Guide*. They hosted a syndicated radio call-in show, *West Coast Garden Live*, heard weekly by more than a million people, and published *Garden Compass* magazine.

Ben Segawa also returned to San Diego from Poston. He was one of the first Japanese Americans to enlist in the United States Air Force, concluding his service with a two-year tour with the United Nations peacekeeping forces in Okinawa. He then farmed with his brother George in Mission Valley until about 1958. After retiring from farming, Ben Segawa co-owned a horticultural supply company. He was a leader in the agricultural community. Even after retirement, he continued to write articles for local agricultural trade magazines. His son Randy became a workplace risk evaluator for the California Department of Pesticide Regulation.

The Balboa Park Tea Pavilion fell into disrepair and was vandalized with anti-Japanese graffiti after World War II. The pavilion and garden were dismantled in 1955. Since then, however, Japanese-style gardens have been created in San Diego County to provide serene settings for such diverse places as the 1964 pearl-diving exhibit at SeaWorld, the Golden Door spa in Escondido, the San Diego Tech Center business park in Sorrento Valley, and the courtyard of the Kiku Gardens Senior Housing Project in Chula Vista, where both Moto Asakawa and Ben Segawa played leading roles in the development of this nonprofit.

Balboa Park's Japanese Friendship Garden was initially conceived in 1955 in the *kai-yushike* style. Funding challenges, design changes, and competing visions on how to support the garden created delays. Moto Asakawa was one of the board members who guided its development and financing. Landscape architect Takeo Uesugi was finally able to complete the Friendship Garden in 2015.

Japanese Americans have played a significant role in San Diego County's gardens and agricultural development. Third- and fourth-generation Japanese Americans are no longer constrained by racial prejudice to careers as laborers, farmers, gardeners, and nurserymen, though some have chosen to continue in these professions. Thanks to Alice Waters's Chez Panisse restaurant and other chefs who embraced her enthusiasm for Chino Farm produce, the Chino family farm is probably the most famous farm in America. The Japanese Tea Garden is still a popular attraction in Golden Gate Park in San Francisco. Adapted to fit Western sensibilities, the Japanese-style garden attracts admirers for its beauty, simplicity, and air of spiritual tranquility. Japanese koi ponds, flowering cherries, Japanese maples, and stepping stones are features of many California gardens regardless of their styles.

The Japanese Friendship Garden in San Diego features a koi pond, as do other California gardens in many styles.

# ACKNOWLEDGMENTS

The idea for this book was conceived by Nancy Carol Carter, a board member of the California Garden & Landscape History Society and frequent contributor to its journal, *Eden*. She suggested that CGLHS publish a collection of early articles to commemorate the organization's twenty-fifth anniversary.

When *Eden: Journal of the California Garden & Landscape History Society* was founded in May 1996 it was initially a newsletter with the goal of one day becoming an accessible but scholarly journal on the varied historic landscapes in California and emphasizing elisions in academic writing at the time. Today *Eden* is beautifully produced, but in the early days due to costs and technology, the graphics were poor, and few images were in color. A book would be a chance to publish enhanced images and update the essays, as well as showcase a sample of landscapes and significant designers from throughout the state. An editorial committee was formed to select essays from the first twenty years of *Eden* that span a range of designed and vernacular cultural landscapes in California. The committee was chaired by Christine Edstrom O'Hara, who read every past *Eden* issue. Other members were Kelly Comras, Steven Keylon, Ann Scheid, and Susan Chamberlin. Twenty-two essays were selected and shortened by the original authors (with help from the coeditors). The essays showcase landscapes representing a range of time periods and geographic areas in California.

As the organization's founder, William A. "Bill" Grant, discovered while doing research for his Spring 1995 *Pacific Horticulture* article on the "Padre of the Roses," historians had challenges finding resources and documentation for West Coast gardens. Grant, a rosarian who taught English at Cabrillo College, decided to do something about it. He and Don Gholston, Librarian at the University of California Santa Cruz Arboretum (where Grant was the president of the Arboretum's Board of Governors) placed notices in several publications for a meeting to be held on September 23, 1995 at the Arboretum

Above Left: David C. Streatfield in Seattle in 2022. Above Right: Top row from the left: California Garden and Landscape History Society founder Bill Grant, John Blocker and Eden editor Marlea Graham. Bottom row: Susan Chamberlin, Vice President Laurie Hannah, Lucy Warren, Margaret Mori, and President Mitzi VanSant, 1999.

*"Here is a part of the world to which people come with the avowed purpose of living out of doors at every season of the year. Life is planned with this idea in view. Houses are designed for it and the garden often assumes a place equal to or more important than that of the house because so much time is spent there."*

—Winifred Starr Dobyns, *California Gardens*, 1931

for anyone interested in creating an organization devoted to California garden history. Twenty-eight individuals attended the meeting. They represented a wide array of interests including landscape architecture and design, garden writers, nursery owners, botanical librarians and garden directors, amateur and professional gardeners, and Grant's rosarian friends. Other founding members joined at the second organizational meeting held in February 1996 at the Santa Barbara Botanic Garden hosted by its librarian, Laurie Hannah, and Virginia Gardner, proprietor of VLT Gardner Horticultural & Botanical Books. To acknowledge cultural landscapes, the name the California Garden & Landscape History Society was adopted. Bill excitedly shared his conviction that the organization should have a journal named *Eden*.

David C. Streatfield, then Department Chair and Professor of Landscape Architecture at University of Washington, gave the keynote address entitled, "The History of Gardens and Landscapes in California." It was a call to action. Streatfield described what CGLHS could accomplish and noted that gardens, "are among human society's greatest creative achievements."[1] However, large areas of scholarship for California landscapes were missing. Lacunae included vernacular landscapes, farm landscapes, large-scale irrigation projects, highways, parks and public open spaces, cemeteries, amusement parks, resorts hotels, and university and college campuses. He identified important landscape architects and designers who needed monographs such as John McLaren, Bruce Porter, Ralph Cornell, Katherine Bashford, Fred Barlow Jr., Ruth Shellhorn, Lawrence Halprin, Robert Royston, Douglas Baylis, and Courtland Paul. Streatfield pointed out that the study of garden history was relatively recent, challenging, and required interdisciplinary research uniting techniques drawn from art history, horticulture, landscape architecture, intellectual and social history, and geography.

The transcript of Streatfield's address was included as an insert in the first issue of *Eden*, which was edited by Bill Grant. He wrote, the purpose of the society was to "record the past, preserve the present, and educate others to carry on the work" with its mission to "identify and conserve, educate and celebrate California's garden and landscape history."[2]

Marlea Graham, who edited the *Rose Letter* for the Heritage Roses Group, volunteered to be the production editor for the newsletter in 1997 with Graham becoming sole editor in 1998. Phoebe Cutler contributed the first work of scholarship to *Eden*, Laurie Hannah did most of the paperwork for our nonprofit status, Lucy Warren organized the first, full CGLHS conference, and Susan Chamberlin founded the website, cglhs.org. A new organization was well on its way. Membership included Californians and others with shared interests from Canada, England, and Australia.

From a humble newsletter to a professionally edited journal, *Eden* has evolved into a publication which is both as satisfying to lay people as it is to scholars. *Eden* editors Marlea Graham, Barbara Marinacci, Virginia Kean, and Steven Keylon have guided the journal and its many authors over the past decades, and CGLHS has them to thank for its excellence. And after nearly thirty years of publication, *Eden* has filled many of the elisions identified by Streatfield in his 1996 address. CGLHS was a 2023 recipient of the Governor's Historic Preservation Award for outstanding achievement in historic preservation, sponsored by the California Office of Historic Preservation and California State Parks.

Members of the California Garden & Landscape History Society supported the development of this book with generous contributions from Nancy Carol Carter, Brent Harris and Lisa Meulbroek, Jaime and Joe Hendrickson, JC Miller, Susan O'Sullivan, and an anonymous donor. The contributors donated their essays and images. Grateful acknowledgment is made for their faith in this endeavor and for adapting their essays originally published in *Eden: Journal of the California Garden & Landscape History Society*: Laura Ackley, John Blocker, Julie Cain, Nancy Carol Carter, Kelly Comras, Phoebe Cutler, Marlea Graham, Steven Keylon, David A. Laws, H. Ray McKnight, Keith Park, Ann Scheid, Paul Scolari, Desmond Smith, Lee Somerville, David C. Streatfield, and the late Harold Tokmakian. Thomas Bassett, the executor for the late Thomas A. Brown, permitted us to adapt Brown's essay, and just before he died, Russell A. Beatty approved our edit of his essay.

Carol Bornstein, Kelly Comras, Marlea Graham, Steven Keylon, Joel Michaelsen, Patrick O'Hara, Keith Park, Libby Simon, and staff at several archives were especially helpful in answering questions and sorting out details. In addition to our spouses for their unfailing encouragement and the wonderful support at Angel City Press and the book's designer, J. Eric Lynxwiler, we would like to acknowledge and thank the following people. Please forgive us for any unintended omissions.

—Susan Chamberlin and Christine Edstrom O'Hara

Antonia Adezio
Rebecca Anderson
Marie Barnidge-McIntyre
Richard Barry
Hannah Barton
Virginia Bones
Marion Brenner
Barbara Briggs-Anderson
Marc Campos
Julianne Burton-Carvajal
Pat Chesnut
Lynda Corey Claassen
Michele Clark
Donald Clinton
Paul Clinton
Robert Clinton
Rachel Cobb
Kelly Crawford
Ann de Forest
Elizabeth de Forest II
Kellam de Forest
Pinky and Don Eastman
Derrik Eichelberger
Ward Eldredge
Natalie Fiocre
Marc Fleishhacker
Terri Garst
Zach Goldsmith
Bob Gordon
Al Graham
Marlea Graham,
    *Eden* editor from 1997 to 2009

William A. "Bill" Grant,
    late founder of California Garden
    & Landscape History Society and
    *Eden* founding editor
Michael Green
Rebecca Hagen
Mick Hales
John Hanna
Laurie Hannah
Millicent Harvey
Saxon Holt
Judy Horton
Robin Karson
Tina Kistinger
Cuong Le
Nadia Leyman
Jonathan Lippincott
Adela Lisanti
Virginia Kean,
    *Eden* editor from 2013 to 2017
Steven Keylon,
    *Eden* editor from 2017 to present
Joseph Marek
Barbara Marinacci,
    *Eden* editor from 2009 to 2013
Christin Markmann
Jason Miller
Samantha Mills
Stephen Morton
Maria Mowrey
Erin Newman
Daisy Njoku
Liam O'Donoghue
Michael O'Hara

Gordon Osmundson
Lorraine Osmundson
Lisa Palella
Paul Penna
Barbara E. Perkins
Peggy Perry
Ryan Pettigrew
Nancy Goslee Power
Alanna Quann
Shannon Quinn
Edwin Rodriguez Jr.
Josh Schneider
Darrell g.h. Schramm
Craig S. Simpson
Natalia Snoyman
Gary Spradlin
Margo Stipe
Tim Street-Porter
Melissa Scroggins
Monique Sugimoto
Julie Tanaka
Rose Thomas
Nils Timm
Robin Tokmakian
Jim Tranquada
Matt Walla
John Walther
Glenn Wenzel
Maxwell Zupke

Overleaf: A trail through the Anza-Borrego Desert State Park with yellow brittlebush (*Encelia farinosa*) in bloom.

# IMAGE CREDITS

Unless noted below, the images in the book come from the authors' collections.

Ann Scheid Collection: 121; 124

Bill Grant Collection: 208, Right

Bornstein, Carol: 14; 157

Brenner, Marion: 28; 42; for The Annenberg Foundation Trust at Sunnylands: 10

California State Library: 22, Left

California State Parks: 179

Carter, Nancy Carol: 112, Below

Chamberlin, Susan: 15, Right; 16; 22, Center; 24, Left; 30; 32; 52; 70; 81; 82; 84; 86; 89; 126; 145; 181, Above; 181, Below Right; 184; 194; 198, 224

Clinton, Donald: 161, Left

Comras, Kelly: 102, Right; 103, Below

Crocker, Bruce 77

Crocker Art Museum: 197

Culter, Phoebe: 160, Left; 160, Right

Cypress Lawn Heritage Foundation: 128, Below; 130

Davis, Timothy: 164

Family of Katherine Bashford: 74, Bottom Left

Fleishhacker Family and Green Gables LLC : 46

Fletcher, Robert M.: 107

Frank Lloyd Wright Foundation: 80, Right

Fred Barlow, Jr. Archives: 74, Bottom Right; 75, Left; 76 78

Ganna Walska Lotusland: 20

Glenn Wenzel Collection: 159, Right

Graham, Marlea: 136; 196; 200

Grant, William A.: 38; 39

Gruen Associates: 162, Right

Hales, Mick: 12, 218

Hanna, John: 80, Left; 85; 88

The Huntington Library, San Marino, California: 74, Above

Japanese American Historical Society of San Diego: 202; 204

Johnson, Kevin: 106

Julian P. Graham/Loonhill Studios: 147

Kaiser Permanente Heritage Resources: 168, Left

Keuser, Harry: 101

Laura A. Ackley Collection: 140; 142, Left; 142, Center; 142, Right; 143; 144, Above; 144, Below

Laws, David A.: 6, 174; 186; 189; 190; 191, Above; 192; 195, Left

Library of American Landscape History: 55

Library of Congress, Prints and Photographs Division, Frances Benjamin Johnston Photograph Collection: 56, 119; Right; Bain Collection: 149; Edward S. Curtis Collection: 152; 176

Liepa, Susan: 72

Los Angeles Public Library, Lucille Stewart Collection: 159, Left

Michaelsen, Joel: 18; 21; 25; 34; 36; 40; 48; 51, Center; 79; 153; 154

Millicent Harvey Photography: 4; 156, Right

Monterey History and Art Association, Mayo Hayes O'Donnell Library: 193

Monterey Museum of Art; Gift of Mrs. J.R. Barker: 191, Below

Morton, Stephen W.: 146

National Park Service, Eugene O'Neill National Historic Site: 90; 91, Above; 91, Below Left; 91, Below Right; 94; 95

Nevada County Historical Society, Searls Historical Library: 33; 35

Occidental College Special Collections and College Archives, Occidental College Photographic Collection: 68, Left; Marc Campos: 68, Right; 69

Osbomb, Richard Barrt: 117, Left

Osmundson, Lorraine: 168, Center

O'Hara, Patrick: 208, Left

Palos Verdes Library District Local History Collection: 47, Right; 50; 51, Right; 54, Below

Rachel Cobb Photography and Design: 110; 114, 115, 205, 207

RHAA Landscape Architects, Douglas Nelson: 165; 166

Richard Nixon Presidential Library and Museum: 116

San Diego History Center: 112, Above; 117, Right

San Francisco History Center, San Francisco Public Library: 141

San José State University Special Collections and Archives: 203, Above; 203, Below

Santa Barbara Botanic Garden: 63, 71

Santa Barbara Historical Museum: 23

Saxon Holt/PhotoBotanic: 2; 7; 57, Below; 60; 66; 92; 96; 99; 118; 120; 122; 125; 127; 132; 133; 134; 137; 139; 156, Left; 167, Below; 169, Left; 170; 171; 182, 212, endpapers

Schulenburg, Frank: 178

Simmonds, Douglas M.: 02, Left; 103, Above

Simon, Libby: 161, Right

Smithsonian Institution, Archives of American Gardens: 56, Left; Garden Club of America Collection: 75, Right

Street-Porter, Tim: 24, Right

Timm, Nils 43; 44

Trotter Galleries, Inc.: 195, Right

U.S. Department of Agriculture, National Agricultural Library, Henry G. Gilbert Nursery and Seed Trade Catalog Collection: 17, Right

United States Department of the Interior, National Park Service, Frederick Law Olmsted National Historic Site: 47, Left; 47, Center; 54, Above; 148, Above; 148, Below; 50

University of California, Berkeley, Bancroft Library: 15, left, 188; Environmental Design Archives, Beatrix Farrand Collection 1955-2: 64; 65, Above; 65, Below; Garrett Eckbo Collection: 162, Left; Robert B. Honeyman Jr. Collection of Early Californian and Western Pictorial Material: 128, Above; Theodore Osmundson Collection: 167, Above; 168, Right; 169, Right

University of California, Berkeley, Environmental Design Archives, UCLA, Charles E. Young Research Library, Special Collections, Los Angeles Times Photographic Archive: 158; Ruth P. Shellhorn papers: 100; 104; 105

University of California, San Diego, Special Collections and Archives: 199

University of Southern California Libraries and California Historical Society: 177

University of Wyoming, American Heritage Center, Victor Gruen Papers: 163

Walla, Matt: 58

# NOTES

## INTRODUCTION

1 Drawing upon multiple sources and decades of research, M. Kat Anderson places Indigenous California protoagriculture between plant gathering and full domestication in the continuum of human-plant interactions. See Anderson's *Tending the Wild: Native American Knowledge and the Management of California's Natural Resources* (Berkeley, CA: University of California Press, 2005). Kent G. Lightfoot and Otis Parrish in *California Indians and their Environment* (Berkeley, CA: University of California Press, 2009) define and examine pyrodiversity resulting from prescribed burns.

2 Scholars now call this period the California Genocide. See for example, Benjamin Madley, *An American Genocide: The United States and the California Indian Catastrophe 1846-1873* (New Haven: Yale University Press, 2016) and Damon B. Akins and William J. Bauer Jr. *We Are the Land: A History of Native California* (Oakland: University of California Press, 2021).

3 In horticultural terms, exotic means a plant that is not native, but exotic can also mean strikingly unusual. We use it both ways.

4 Charles Gibbs Adams, Victoria Padilla, Carey McWilliams, Harry M. Butterfield, David C. Streatfield, Jere Stuart French, and Thomas A. Brown are early scholars of the California landscape. Architectural historians Esther McCoy, David Gebhard, Robert Winter, and Reyner Banham often included landscape in their writings.

5 Harry M. Butterfield, "Dates of Introduction of Trees and Shrubs to California" (U.C Davis: unpublished manuscript, 1964); Judith M. Taylor M.D. and the late Harry M. Butterfield, *Tangible Memories: Californians and Their Gardens 1800–1950.* (Xlibris Corporation, 2003).

6 There have been many changes to the garden since Walska died. It is now a non-profit botanical garden called Ganna Walska Lotusland.

7 See for example J.B. Jackson's journal, *Landscape*, his books, and his collections of essays. The Secretary of the Interior's Standards for the Treatment of Historic Properties now recognize four general types of cultural landscapes: historic vernacular landscapes, historic designed landscapes, historic sites, and ethnographic landscapes.

8 David C. Streatfield, "An Address on the History of Gardens and Landscapes in California," *Eden* 1, no. 1 (May 1996): 1.

## PART 1

## INTRODUCTION

1 David Streatfield, *California Gardens: Creating a New Eden* (New York: Abbeville Press, 1994), 154, 176.

## THE EMPIRE COTTAGE IN GRASS VALLEY: WILLIAM B. BOURN JR., WILLIS POLK, AND OSCAR PRAGER

1 William B. Ingalls to Abbott Ingalls, 25 August 1903, in Ferol Egan, *Last Bonanza Kings* (Reno, NV: University of Nevada Press, 1998), 266.

2 Agnes Bourn to Sarah Bourn, 23 September 1903, Box 11, William Bowers Bourn family papers, Bancroft Library, University of California, Berkeley. In addition to consulting primary sources in the Bancroft library, original research was conducted in the Environmental Design Archives at the University of California, Berkeley.

## THE LANDSCAPE AT GREEN GABLES

1 This essay is an excerpt from David C. Streatfield, "The San Francisco Peninsula's Great Estates: Part II, "*Eden*, Spring 2012, 1-17. Much of the material combines information, insights, and opinions given in passages of articles written by the author that previously appeared in his book, *California Gardens: Creating a New Eden*, and in three earlier published articles, "Echoes of England and Italy 'on the edge of the world': Green Gables and Charles Greene," "'Paradise' on the Frontier: Victorian Gardens on the San Francisco Peninsula" and "Where Pine and Palm Meet: the California Garden as a Regional Expression." (See full citations in the Bibliography.)

2 Charles Sumner Greene, Planting design specifications (Unpublished, Private collection of Fleishhacker Family, c. 1928), 4.

## A RADICAL VISION FOR PALOS VERDES

1 Olmsted Brothers's correspondence and plans note this community as the Palos Verdes Project as well as Palos Verdes Estates. However, at that time, what is now Miraleste in Rancho Palos Verdes was part of the initial design. In 1939, the northwest section of the community incorporated into Palos Verdes Estates which can be confusing to the reader. For this essay, I will use "Palos Verdes" to describe the original sixteen thousand acres, later reduced to three thousand, two hundred acres, that were designed between 1914–1930.

2 Dwight L. Oliver, *Landscape Architecture, Frederick Law Olmsted, Jr. and Frederick Law Olmsted, Sr.: Extraordinary Careers* (Oakhurst, California: Nelson Press, 1991), 7.

3 According to Susan L. Klaus in "All in the Family: The Olmsted Office and the Business of Landscape Architecture," *Landscape Journal* 16, no. 1 (Spring 1997), when John Charles Olmsted died in 1920, Olmsted Jr. maintained the Olmsted Brothers name "both for sentimental and business reasons, believing that the many changes in the name of the Olmsted office in the past were rather unfortunate" in preserving the firm's historical identity (Olmsted Jr. to Arthur C. Comey, March 24, 1920, Records of the Olmsted Associates, Manuscript Room at the Library of Congress).

4 Draft of Proposed Contingent Agreement between Olmsted Brothers and the Trustee, October 9, 1922. Contract. From Library of Congress, Records of the Olmsted Associates, Manuscript Room at Library of Congress.

5 See Christine Edstrom O'Hara, "The Panama-California Exposition, San Diego, 1915: The Olmsted Brothers' Ecological Park Typology," *Journal for the Society of Architectural Historians* 7, no. 1 (March 2011): 64-81.

6 Describing that work to W.H. Kiernan, Vanderlip's Western representative, Olmsted Brothers wrote that the plantsman [Horner] was "to study local plants and conditions and to collect and raise nursery stock chiefly of hardy native kinds of shrubs and trees requiring little or no care after they are established for restoring the beauty of arroyos and precipitous hillsides which have become more or less bare and ugly in some places owing to pasturing, fires and other interference by man." (John Charles Olmsted. Letter to Kiernan, 25 September 1914, Job #5950, Records of the Olmsted Associates, Manuscript Room at Library of Congress.)

7 John Charles Olmsted to W.H. Kiernan, October 19, 1914. Letter. From Library of Congress, Records of the Olmsted Associates, Manuscript Room at Library of Congress.

8 Palos Verdes Homes Association calls this park Farnham Martin, whereas Olmsted Brothers called it Farnham Martin's.

## LOCKWOOD DE FOREST, ASLA, AND THE SANTA BARBARA LANDSCAPE

1 Lockwood de Forest Jr., "Do Lawns Belong in Southern California Gardens?" *Garden and Homebuilder* 40 (December 1924): 232.

2 De Forest didn't specify scientific names for these common natives. There are many useful species of *Ceanothus*. The others are probably *Heteromeles arbutifolia* (California Holly, Christmas-berry, or toyon), *Prunus ilicifolia* and/or *P.i. lyonia* (wild cherries), *Malosma laurina* (sumac or possibly lemonadeberry, *Rhus integrifolia*), and *Rhamnus californica* (coffeeberry).

3 De Forest's parents were Meta Kemble de Forest (1852-1953), an unconventional du Pont descendant, and Lockwood de Forest II or Sr. (1850-1932) a distinguished artist, author, and one-time partner of Louis Comfort Tiffany. Also known as Lockwood de Forest III, the landscape architect de Forest used "Jr." as his professional name.

4 "Spanish Flu" and "no imagination" Kellam de Forest to author, April-May 2014 conversations and emails.

5 David Gebhard, introduction to Rebecca Conard, Christopher H. Nelson, Mary Louise Days, *Santa Barbara: A Guide to El Pueblo Viejo* (Santa Barbara CA: Capra Press, 1986), 12.

6 David C. Streatfield, "The Garden at Casa del Herrero," *Antiques* 130, no. 2 (August 1986): 286-293. Molly Barker, Susan Chamberlin, Robert L. Sweeney, "National Historic Landmark Nomination: Steedman Estate/ Casa del Herrero", 2008. For the lifestyle of the maverick de Forests, see Trish Reynales, "The Naturals: Elizabeth and Lockwood de Forest," *Santa Barbara Magazine* (Summer 1995): 42-49.

7 David C. Streatfield, *California Gardens: Creating a New Eden* (New York: Abbeville Press, 1994), 177. Both house and garden have been altered.

8 *Santa Barbara New-Press,* "Lockwood de Forest, Landscape Architect, Dies," (Santa Barbara, CA) March 30, 1949, A-1. Edward Huntsman-Trout, "A Biographical Minute," *Landscape Architecture* (1949): 35.

9 Robin Karson, *A Genius for Place* (Amherst, MA: University of Massachusetts Press, 2007), 283, note 68 credits David Streatfield for this idea.

### BEATRIX FARRAND IN SOUTHERN CALIFORNIA, 1925–1959

1 Editors' note: Diana Balmori says Farrand "landscaped" Casa Dorinda on page 186 of *Beatrix Farrand's American Landscapes: Her Gardens and Campuses.* However, letters in the Montecito History Committee archive and an article in the January 1921 edition of *Architectural Forum* clearly establish Riedel as the landscape architect for the estate with site plan by its architect, C.W. Winslow Sr. Later consultations were also minor. See Susan Chamberlin, "Beatrix Farrand in Santa Barbara, 1925–1959," *Eden* 14, no. 2 (Spring 2011): 15–19. A detailed 1918 plan described in the letters (and believed lost) was recently donated by the Riedel-Preuss family to the Edson Smith Collection at the Santa Barbara Public Library. This essay has been edited for length and clarity and includes information from Chamberlin, "Beatrix Farrand in Santa Barbara."

2 Yale President J.R. Angell to Max Farrand. Max Farrand Papers, Huntington Library Archives.

3 Max Farrand to Caltech President R.A. Millikan, May 8, 1929. Millikan Papers, Caltech Archives.

4 BF to G.E. Hale, March 8, 1928. George Ellery Hale Papers, Caltech Archives. Included were design and planting specifications. The Hale Solar Laboratory is now a National Historic Landmark.

5 Information on Caltech's architecture and landscape is drawn from Romy Wyllie's book, *Caltech's Architectural Heritage*, (Glendale: Balcony Press, 2000) and from conversations with Wyllie.

6 Millikan Papers, Caltech Archives.

7 R.A. Millikan to BF, Sept. 18, 1938. Millikan Papers, Caltech Archives.

8 BF to RAM, Nov. 16, 1938. Millikan Papers, Caltech Archives.

9 Occidental President Remsen D. Bird to BF, Nov. 11, 1936. Fred F. McClain files, Special Collections, Occidental College Library. Unless otherwise noted, all Occidental College sources cited are found in two file folders kept by Comptroller Fred F. McClain and now in Special Collections.

10 BF to McLain, June 14, 1938.

11 BF to H.C. Chambers, Oct. 28, 1937.

12 BF to McLain, Dec. 3, 1937: "The Britannia Seat is one which they have made from a design of mine. . ."

13 Change order, H.C. Chambers to Hollingsworth, general contractor, Dec. 6, 1937.

14 BF to Hunt and Chambers, Aug. 31, 1939.

15 BF to AB, April 3, 1940.

16 For example, a 2018 documentary film, "The Life and Gardens of Beatrix Farrand" directed by Karyl Evans, names only Farrand when the Santa Barbara Botanic Garden is mentioned.

17 RB to MF, March 18, 1941. Huntington Library Archives.

18 BF to Mrs. Robert Gordon Sproul, March 31, 1941. Huntington Library Archives.

### THE CALIFORNIA LANDSCAPES OF KATHERINE BASHFORD

1 Nellie Van de Grift Sanchez, *California and Californians*, (Chicago: The Lewis Publishing Company, 1926), 203.

2 Though it has been commonly believed that Bashford began her career apprenticing with Florence Yoch, Pasadena City Directories list her as landscape architect or landscape gardener beginning in 1917. Bashford even placed her name in the Landscape Architects section in the 1917 LA City Directory, along with Wilbur Cook, Charles Gibbs Adams, and A.E. Hanson.

3 After graduating from Marlborough, Bashford is said to have attended classes at Polytechnic High School, which by 1914 was offering courses in architecture, the curriculum being provided by the Society of Beaux-Arts Architects of America. She also later studied art at the Otis Art Institute, as did Mabel Alvarez.

4 Van de Grift Sanchez, *California and Californians,* 12.

5 David C. Streatfield (professor emeritus of the Landscape Architecture Department at the University of Washington), e-mail to author, December 21, 2010.

6 Richardson Little Wright and Robert Stell Lemmon, "California's Gardens Cling to Their Spanish Ancestry," *House and Garden's Second Book of Gardens* (New York: Condé Nast Publications, 1927), 34.

7 Katherine Bashford, "A Course in the Appreciation of Architecture: The Relation of House to Garden," *California Southland* (April 1926), 28.

8 Katherine Bashford "Two Little Gardens," *California Southland* (January 1924), 8.

9 Father Bede Reynolds, *A Rebel From Riches* (Milford, Ohio: The Riehle Foundation, 1984), 80.

10 Helen W. King, "In a Canyon, Too. But This Garden is an Informal One," *Los Angeles Times* (Los Angeles, CA), April 9, 1933.

11 The only other landscape architect in the building was the esteemed Charles Gibbs Adams.

12 Dr. Samuel Stillman Berry to Katherine Bashford, November 10, 1932 in Smithsonian Institution Archives, Record Unit 7335, Box 6 of 15, S. Stillman Berry Papers, 1880-1984.

13 Katherine Bashford to Dr. Samuel Stillman Berry, July 12, 1933 in Smithsonian Institution Archives, Record Unit 7335, Box 6 of 15, S. Stillman Berry Papers, 1880-1984.

14 Arthur G. Barton, "A Biographical Minute," *Landscape Architecture Quarterly*, XLIV, no. 1 (October, 1953), 29.

15 Fred Barlow Jr., "Palm Springs Gardens," *California Arts & Architecture*, February 1937, 32.

16 Fred Barlow Jr., "Palm Springs Gardens," *California Arts & Architecture*, February 1937, 32.

### A PLAYWRIGHT'S GARDEN: EUGENE O'NEILL'S TAO HOUSE

1 Michael Hankinson, "Cultural Landscape Report—Eugene O'Neill National Historic Site."(National Park Service, 2004, excerpted from a letter by Eugene O'Neill to Barrett Clark, September 14, 1937), 91.

2 Hankinson, "Cultural Landscape Report," Appendix C.

3 Hankinson, "Cultural Landscape Report," excerpted from the diaries of Carlotta Monterey O'Neill, 1938-1943, 237.

4 Hankinson, "Cultural Landscape Report," 99.

5 Hankinson, "Cultural Landscape Report", 19.

6 Hankinson, "Cultural Landscape Report," Appendix C.

7 Hankinson, "Cultural Landscape Report," Appendix C.

8 Hankinson, "Cultural Landscape Report," Appendix C.

9 Hankinson, "Cultural Landscape Report," 101.

10 Hankinson, "Cultural Landscape Report", 25.

11 Cathy A. Gilbert, *The Tao House Courtyard: Historic Landscape Study and Design Proposal*, 1986, Appendix.

### RUTH PATRICIA SHELLHORN, FASLA (1909–2006)

1 This essay is based upon excerpts from two *Eden* articles, as well as research for *Ruth Shellhorn* by Kelly Comras.

## PART 2

### BORDER FIELD STATE PARK AND ITS MONUMENT

1 Ralph Bennett, "Border Field Becomes State Park,"*Evening Tribune* (San Diego, CA), August 18, 1971, 1; "U.S. Land Made State Border Park," *San Diego Union* (San Diego, CA), August 19, 1971, 13.

2 U.S. Army Engineer District, Los Angeles, California. Tijuana River Flood Control Channel Project Draft Environmental Statement, 1971, San Diego, 1972, 14, 38.

3 Tijuana River National Estuarine Research Reserve, "About TRNERR," https://trnerr.org/about/ (accessed January 16, 2023).

### THE LEGACY OF PASADENA'S TREES

1 Queen palms were formerly named *Cocos plumosa* and *Arecastrum romanzoffianum.*

### CYPRESS LAWN AND THE RURAL CEMETERY MOVEMENT

1 The late author was a consultant to Cypress Lawn Memorial Park and the rehabilitation of its historic East Campus. This essay was condensed from his essay in *Eden*, which in turn was based on his much longer, 2002 "Historic Landscape Report" for the cemetery where citations and bibliography can be found.

### JOHN MCLAREN: LANDSCAPE MAGICIAN OF SAN FRANCISCO'S 1915 EXPOSITION

1 "Interesting Westerners," *Sunset* (1913): 1215.

2 John McLaren, "California's Opportunities in Artistic Landscaping," *California's Magazine*, 2 (1916): 139.

3 "John McLaren's Work at the Exposition Entitles Him to the Name of Magic Gardener," *San Francisco Chronicle* (San Francisco, CA), Jan. 12, 1916: 39; Leonard Carpenter, "Panama-Pacific Exposition: Some of the Horticultural Features," *The American Florist*, Aug. 14, 1915: 149.

4 Frank Morton Todd, *The Story of the Exposition* (New York: G.P. Putnam's Sons, 1921), 161.

5 McLaren, "California's Opportunities": 140; Donald McLaren, "Landscape Gardening at the Exposition," *Pacific Coast Architect*, (July 1915): 13.

6 Alice McGowan, "Exposition's Pastel City a Dream of Soft Color," *New York Tribune* (New York City, NY), Feb. 14, 1915: 3; "John McLaren's Work at the Exposition Entitles Him to the Name of Magic Gardener," *San Francisco Chronicle* (San Francisco, CA), Jan. 12, 1916: 39.

7 McLaren, "California's Opportunities": 140.

### LAPD'S ROCK GARDEN

1 "Police Build West Point: Elysian Park Retreat Realization for Better Officers," *Los Angeles Times* (Los Angeles, CA), August 28, 1983. According to the LAPRAAC website, the facility was removed from the jurisdiction of the Parks and Recreation Department in a 1972 ballot measure, so it is no longer technically in the boundaries of Elysian Park and is instead managed by the Department of Public Works.

2 Andrew Meieran, a local entrepreneur, bought Clifton's in 2017 and has renovated it more than once. At the time of this writing,

it has several floors with different dining and drinking options, and some of the original, fantastical décor still exists.

3  F. Scotti to R.P. Butchart, February 28, 1930 letter in the Butchart Gardens archive.

4  For further reading on Clifford Clinton's life, see a biography by his grandson: Edmond J. Clinton III, *Clifton's and Clifford Clinton: A Cafeteria and a Crusader* (Los Angeles: Angel City Press, 2015).

## GARRETT ECKBO'S FULTON MALL

1  Editors' Note: This essay was originally written in 2013 and chronicled the history of Fulton Mall, arguing for its preservation. As the mall was demolished in 2016, editing changed the essay to past tense as this landscape no longer exists.

2  See "ParkScore Index," Trust for Public Land, https://www.tpl.org/parkscore, Accessed March 2013

3  Garrett Eckbo, Laura Lawson, Walter Hood, and Chip Sullivan, *People in a Landscape* (Upper Saddle River, NJ: Prentice Hall, 1998), 190.

4  City of Fresno, "City of Fresno Celebrates the Grand Re-Opening of Fulton Street," October 21, 2017, https://www.fresno.gov/news/city-of-fresno-celebrates-the-grand-re-opening-of-fulton-street/, (accessed July 23, 2022).

## MID-CENTURY MODERN: THE KAISER ROOF GARDEN COMES OF AGE

1  Theodore Osmundson, Jr. "Kaiser Center Roof Garden," *Landscape Architecture* 53, no. 1 (October 1962): 15.

2  Jenny Strasburg, "Gardens in the Sky," *San Francisco Examiner* (San Francisco, CA), December 5, 1999: D-1, D-3; Cornell Maier (Kaiser executive) oral history interview

with Chris Patillo and Marlea Graham for the Historic American Landscape Survey (HALS), February 1, 2007.

3  Edgar J. Kaiser Papers, MSS 85/61c, Kaiser Center, Inc., Files. Carton 132:15. Bancroft Library, University of California at Berkeley; David Arbegast (landscape architect), oral history interview with Chris Patillo and Marlea Graham for HALS, August 1, 2006.

4  Arbegast, Oral History.

5  Johnson C. Sue (landscape architect), oral history interview with Chris Patillo and Marlea Graham for HALS, November 1, 2006.

6  Sue, Oral History.

7  Deborah Lindsey (Kaiser garden consultant) in discussion with the author, ~2008–2009.

## PART 3

### SONOMA COUNTY'S LANDSCAPE HISTORY

1  Editors' Note: M. Kat Anderson, *Tending the Wild: Native American Knowledge and the Management of California's Natural Resources* (Berkeley, CA: University of California Press, 2004) synthesizes decades of knowledge on the topic. For more specifics on plants, pyrodiversity from prescribed burns, and agriculture including how the Coast Miwok transplanted small California bay trees, see Kent G. Lightfoot and Otis Parrish, *California Indians and their Environment* (Berkeley, CA: University of California Press, 2009.)The article upon which this essay is based has been edited for length and clarity. Additional information from recent scholarship, such as Benjamin Madley, *An American Genocide* (New Haven: Yale University Press, 2016) and Damon B. Akins and William J. Bauer Jr., *We Are the Land* (Oakland, CA: Univer-

sity of California Press, 2021) on the "California Genocide" was included, which we believe the late Tom Brown would support because he debunked the romantic mission garden in his work. (He was also an authority on plant introductions.) For a more recent critique of mission gardens, see Elizabeth Kryder-Reid, *California Mission Landscapes* (Minneapolis: University of Minnesota Press, 2016.) Russians at Fort Ross and in Alaska also mistreated Indigenous peoples.

2  Editors' Note: One of the jobs of the troops housed in the barracks Vallejo built was to round up runaway Indigenous workers. Anderson, Tending the Wild, 82; Madley *An American Genocide*, 40. Vallejo is considered by many as an "Indian slaver" today. Edward D. Castillo, "Short Overview of California Indian History," 2022, State of California, Native American Heritage Commission, Sacramento, CA, nahc@nahc.ca.gov (accessed September 2022); Atkins and Bauer Jr., *We are the Land*, 113. Rancho Petaluma is now Petaluma Adobe State Historic Park, and the other Vallejo properties are part of Sonoma State Historic Park.

### JAPANESE GARDENS, AMERICAN GARDENERS IN SAN DIEGO COUNTY

Quotes in this essay are from Kendall H. Brown, *Japanese-Style Gardens of the Pacific West Coast.* (NY: Rizzoli, 1999).

### EPILOGUE

1  David C. Streatfield, "An Address on the History of Gardens and Landscapes in California," *Eden* 1, no. 1 (May 1996): 1.

2  Bill Grant, "A Brief History of CG&LHS," *Eden* 1, no. 1 (May 1996): 2.

# FOR FURTHER READING

Aguar, Charles E., and Berdeana Aguar. *Wrightscapes: Frank Lloyd Wright's Landscape Designs.* New York: McGraw-Hill, 2002.

Akins, Damon B. and William J. Bauer Jr. *We Are the Land: A History of Native California.* Oakland, CA: University of California Press, 2021.

Allen, Rebecca. "Alta California Missions and Pre-1849 Transformations of Coastal Lands." *Historical Archaeology* 44, no. 3 (2010): 69-80.

Anderson, M. Kat. *Tending the Wild: Native American Knowledge and the Management of California's Natural Resources.* Berkeley: University of California Press, 2005.

Austin, David. *The Rose.* Suffolk, UK: Antique Collectors' Club/Garden Art Press, 2009.

Bakker, Elna. *An Island Called California: An Ecological Introduction to its Natural Communities.* Berkeley, CA: University of California Press, 1971.

Barth, Gunther Paul. "The Park Cemetery: Its Westward Migration." In Craig Zabel and Susan Scott Munshower, *American Public Architecture: European Roots and Native Expressions.* University Park, PA: Pennsylvania State University, 1989.

Beatty, Russell A. "Browning of the Greensward." *Pacific Horticulture* 38, no. 3 (Fall 1997): 37-46.

Birnbaum, Charles A. "Preservation Briefs 36, Protecting Cultural Landscapes: Planning, Treatment and Management of Historic Landscapes." Washington, DC: US Department of the Interior, National Park Service, Cultural Resources, 1994.

Brown, Kendall. *Japanese-style Gardens of the Pacific West Coast.* New York: Rizzoli Inc., 1999.

Brown, Thomas A. "Gardens of the California Missions." *Pacific Horticulture* 49, no.1 (Spring 1988): 3-11.

Butterfield, Harry M. "The Introduction of Eucalyptus to California." *Madroño* 3 (1935): 149-154.

Carroll, Mary. "A Garden for All Time: The Santa Barbara Botanic Garden, 1926–2005." *Noticias: Journal of the Santa Barbara Historical Museum* 50, no. 4 & 51, no. 1 (Winter 2004/Spring 2005): 1-65.

Chamberlin, Susan. "Stevens, Ralph T." In *Shaping the American Landscape,* Charles A. Birnbaum and Stephanie S. Foell, eds. Charlottesville, VA: University of Virginia Press, 2009: 333-335.

de Forest, Lockwood, Jr. "Do Lawns Belong in Southern California?" *Garden and Homebuilder* (December 1924): 232.

Deverell, William. *Whitewashed Adobe: The Rise of Los Angeles and the Remaking of its Mexican Past.* Berkeley: University of California Press, 2004.

Dobyns, Winifred Starr with a new Introduction by Carol Greentree. *California Gardens.* Santa Barbara: Allen A. Knoll, 1996.

Dümpelmann, Sonja and John Beardsley, eds. *Women, Modernity, and Landscape Architecture.* London and New York: Routledge, 2015.

Egan, Ferol. *Last Bonanza Kings: The Bourns of San Francisco, 1998.* Reno, NV: University of Nevada, 1998.

Estes, Donald H. "Before the War: The Japanese in San Diego." *The Journal of San Diego History* 24 (Fall 1978): 425-456.

Faragher, John Mack. *California: An American History.* New Haven, CT: Yale University Press, 2022.

Gebhard, David. "The Spanish Colonial Revival in Southern California, 1895-1930." *Journal of the Society of Architectural Historians* 26 (May 1967): 131-147.

———. "Introduction" in A.E. Hanson. *An Arcadian Landscape: The California Gardens of A.E. Hanson: 1920-1932.* David Gebhard and Sheila Lynds, eds. Los Angeles: Hennessey & Ingalls, 1985.

Grate, Frances. "Historic Gardens of Monterey." *Eden* 3, no. 1 (Spring 2000): 1-3.

Greentree, Carol. "World's Fairs and California's Horticultural History Part I." *Eden* 2, no. 1 (Spring 1999): 1-5.

Griswold, Mac, and Eleanor Weller. *The Golden Age of American Gardens: Proud Owners, Private Estates, 1890-1940.* New York: Harry N. Abrams, 1991.

Gutiérrez, Ramón A., and Richard J. Orsi, eds. *Contested Eden: California Before the Gold Rush.*

Berkeley, CA: University of California Press, 1998.

Hardwick, Michael R. *Changes in Landscape: The Beginnings of Horticulture in the California Missions.* Orange, CA: Paragon Agency, 2005.

Hart, James D. *A Companion to California, Revised Edition.* Berkeley: University of California Press, 1987.

Hayden, Dolores. *The Power of Place: Urban Landscapes as Public History.* Cambridge, MA: MIT Press, 1995.

Hayes, Derek. *Historical Atlas of California.* Berkeley: University of California Press, 2007.

Hood, Walter and Grace Mitchell Tada, editors. *Black Landscapes Matter.* Charlottesville: University of Virginia Press, 2020.

Jackson, Helen Hunt, introduction by Denise Chávez. *Ramona.* New York: Modern Library, 2005.

Jackson, John Brinckerhoff. *Discovering the Vernacular Landscape.* New Haven, CT: Yale University Press, 1984.

Jefferson, Alison Rose. *Living the California Dream: African American Leisure Sites During the Jim Crow Era.* Lincoln: University of Nebraska Press, 2020.

Kryder-Reid, Elizabeth. *California Mission Landscapes: Race, Memory, and the Politics of Heritage.* Minneapolis: University of Minnesota Press, 2016.

Lawrence, Henry W. *City Trees: A Historical Geography form the Renaissance through the Nineteenth Century.* Charlottesville, VA: University of Virginia Press, 2006.

Leonard, Kevin Allen. ''Is That What We Fought For: Japanese Americans and Racism in California. The Impact of World War II,''

*Western Historical Quarterly* 21 (November 1990): 463-482.

Lightfoot, Kent G. and Otis Parrish. *California Indians and their Environment: An Introduction.* Berkeley: University of California Press, 2009.

Lindsay, Diana. "History in the California Desert: The Creation of the Anza-Borrego Desert State Park—Largest in the United States." *San Diego Historical Society Quarterly* 19, no. 4 (Fall 1973).

Madley, Benjamin. *An American Genocide: The United States and the California Indian Catastrophe, 1846-1873.* New Haven: Yale University Press, 2016.

Morgan, Delane. *The Palos Verdes Story.* Palos Verdes Peninsula: Palos Verdes Peninsula Library Foundation, 1983.

O'Hara, Christine Edstrom. "Ecological Planning in 1920s California: The Olmsted Brothers's Design of Palos Verdes Estates." *Landscape Journal* 35, no. 2 (2017): 219-235.

O'Malley, Therese and Joachim Wolschke-Bulmahn, eds. *Modernism and Landscape Architecture, 1890-1940.* New Haven, CT: Yale University Press, 2015

Osmundson, Theodore. *Roof Gardens: History, Design, and Construction.* New York: W.W. Norton & Co., 1999.

Padilla, Victoria. *Southern California Gardens: An Illustrated History.* Berkeley and Los Angeles: University of California Press, 1961.

Reisner, Marc postscript by Lawrie Mott. *Cadillac Desert: The American West and its Disappearing Water.* New York: Penguin Books, 1993.

Sackman, Douglas C. *Orange Empire: California and the Fruits of Eden.* Berkeley: University of California Press, 2007.

Silliman, Stephen. *Lost Laborers in Colonial*

*California: Native Americans and the Archaeology of Rancho Petaluma.* Tucson: University of Arizona Press, 2004.

Simo, Melanie Louise and Peter Walker. *Invisible Gardens: The Search for Modernism in the American Landscape.* Cambridge, MA: MIT Press, 1994.

Starr Kevin and Richard J. Orsi, eds. *Rooted in Barbarous Soil: People, Culture, and Community in Gold Rush California.* Berkeley: University of California Press, 2000.

Streatfield, David C. *California Gardens: Creating a New Eden.* New York: Abbeville Press, 1994.

_____. "Where Palm and Pine Meet: The California Garden as a Regional Expression." *Landscape Journal* 4, no. 2 (Fall 1985): 60–74.

_____ . "Echoes of England and Italy 'On the Edge of the World': Green Gables and Charles Greene." *Journal of Garden History* 2, no. 4 (Oct.–Dec. 1982): 377–398.

Tankard, Judith B. *Beatrix Farrand: Private Gardens, Public Landscapes.* New York: Monacelli Press, 2009. (Revised and reissued as *Beatrix Farrand: Garden Artist, Landscape Architect.* New York: Monacelli Press, 2022.)

Taylor, Judith and the late Harry Morton Butterfield. *Tangible Memories: Californians and their Gardens 1800–1950.* Xlibris Corporation, 2003.

Treib, Marc and Dorothée Imbert. *Garrett Eckbo: Modern Landscapes for Living.* Berkeley: University of California Press, 1997.

Way, Thaïsa. *Unbound Practice: Women and Landscape Architecture.* Charlottesville, VA: University of Virginia Press, 2013.

"Police Build West Point: Elysian Park Retreat Realization for Better Officers." *Los Angeles Times* 28 (August 1938).

# BIBLIOGRAPHY

Complete bibliography for *California Eden: Heritage Landscapes of the Golden State* can be found on the California Garden & Landscape History Society website, www.cglhs.org.

The essays in this book were edited by their authors and the coeditors for length and clarity. These are the original, unedited essays as they appeared in *Eden: Journal of the California Garden & Landscape History Society*, archived on the society's website under EDEN:

Ackley, Laura. "John McLaren, Landscape Magician of the 1915 Exposition." *Eden* 18, no. 3 (Summer 2015): 10-12.

Beatty, Russell. "Cypress Lawn & the Rural Cemetery Movement." *Eden* 6, no. 1 (Spring 2003): 1-11.

Blocker, John. "Japanese Gardens, American Gardeners in San Diego County, Part I." *Eden* 10, no. 3 (Fall 2007): 2-6; and "Japanese Gardens, American Gardeners in San Diego County, Part II." *Eden* 10, no. 4 (Winter 2007): 5-9.

Brown, Thomas A. "Sonoma County's Landscape and Horticultural History." *Eden* 15, no. 3 (Summer 2012): 1-11.

Cain, Julie. "Frank Lloyd Wright's Landscape at Hanna House." *Eden* 12, no. 3 (Fall 2009): 1-7.

Carter, Nancy Carol. "Border Field State Park and Its Monument." *Eden* 14, no. 4 (Fall 2011): 11-13.

Chamberlin, Susan. "Lockwood de Forest ASLA and the Santa Barbara Landscape." *Eden* 17, no. 3 (Summer 2014): 4-9; and "Be-

atrix Farrand in Santa Barbara, 1925-1959." *Eden* 14, no. 2 (Spring 2011): 15-19.

Comras, Kelly. "Ruth Shellhorn (1909-2006)." *Eden* 10, no. 1 (Spring 2007): 15-17; and "Ruth Shellhorn's Garden for Dorothy & Norman Chandler." *Eden* 22, no. 1 (Winter 2019): 29-33.

Cutler, Phoebe. "The LAPD Cascade at Elysian Park." *Eden* 17, no. 2 (Spring 2014): 10-14. _____. "Oscar Prager, Willis Polk, and the Empire Mine of Grass Valley." *Eden* 9, no. 1 (Spring 2006): 1-8.

Graham, Marlea. "Mid-Century Modern: The Kaiser Roof Garden Comes of Age." *Eden* 12, no. 2 (Summer 2009): 1-9.

Keylon, Steven. "The California Landscapes of Katherine Bashford." *Eden* 16, no.4 (Fall 2013): 3-13.

Laws, David A. "Garden History of the Monterey Peninsula, Redux." *Eden* 19, no. 4 (Fall 2016): 3-9.

O'Hara, Christine Edstrom. "A Radical Vision

for Palos Verdes Estates: Early Sustainable Planning on the West Coast." *Eden* 19, no. 2 (Spring 2016): 3-7.

Park, Keith and Paul Scolari. "A Playwright's Garden: Eugene O'Neill's Tao House, 1937-2016." *Eden* 19, no. 3 (Summer 2016): 3-9.

Scheid, Ann. "Beatrix Farrand in Southern California." *Eden* 14, no. 2 (Spring 2011): 1-13. _____. "The Legacy of Pasadena's Trees." *Eden* 16, no. 2 (Spring 2013): 4-9.

Smith, Desmond. "Marion Hollins and the Creation of Santa Cruz's Pasatiempo." *Eden* 13, no. 2 (Summer 2010): 24.

Somerville, Lee. "Anza-Borrego Desert State Park." *Eden* 14, no. 4 (Fall 2011): 10.

Streatfield, David S. "Green Gables" in "The San Francisco Peninsula's Great Estates: Part II, Mansions, Landscapes, and Gardens in the Late 19th and early 20th Centuries." *Eden* 15, no. 2 (Spring 2012): 11-12.

Tokmakian, Harold and H. Ray McKnight. "Eckbo's Fulton Mall: The Case for Preservation." *Eden* 16, no. 3 (Summer 2013): 1-6.

# ABOUT THE CONTRIBUTORS

**LAURA ACKLEY** holds graduate degrees from the Harvard University Graduate School of Design and the UC Berkeley College of Environmental Design. Her book, *San Francisco's Jewel City: The Panama-Pacific International Exposition of 1915*, won a Gold Medal at the 2015 California Book Awards, a Bronze Medal for US History from the National Independent Publisher Book Awards, and the Oscar Lewis Award from the San Francisco History Association.

**RUSSELL A. BEATTY**, ASLA, (1936-2022) taught in the Department of Landscape Architecture and Environmental Planning at UC Berkeley for twenty-eight years and served on the Garden Conservancy Screening Committee. He was the author of numerous articles, books, and historic landscape reports including one on Cypress Lawn Cemetery.

**JOHN BLOCKER** retired from the San Diego County Department of Agriculture with over thirty years of service. He is a founding member of the California Garden & Landscape History Society (CGLHS) and writes a horticultural history column "Growing Grounds" for *California Garden* magazine.

**THOMAS A. BROWN**, ASLA, (1932-2012) earned an MLA from UC Berkeley and founded his own firm in Petaluma in 1974, specializing in historic landscape research and restoration. He also lectured in landscape history in the UC Berkeley Extension program and was a past president of CGLHS.

**JULIE CAIN** is a historian and the Historic Preservation Planner for Heritage Services at Stanford University. She is interested in nineteenth century California history with an emphasis on San Francisco Peninsula landscapes, the role of Chinese immigrants within the state, and the development of Stanford University.

**NANCY CAROL CARTER** is a San Diego historian focused on landscape and gardens, Balboa Park, Kate O. Sessions, and regional horticulture. She holds MS, MLS, and JD degrees and is retired from the University of San Diego School of Law.

**SUSAN CHAMBERLIN**, ASLA, is a landscape historian with a degree in Landscape Architecture from UC Berkeley and an MA in Architectural Histo-

ry from UC Santa Barbara. She is a founding member of CGLHS and has lectured, taught landscape history, and contributed to books, journals, and historic resources reports.

**KELLY COMRAS**, FASLA, is a licensed landscape architect and attorney in California. She is a founding member of The Cultural Landscape Foundation's Stewardship Council, and past president of CGLHS. She has lectured at Harvard GSD, Society of Architectural Historians, California Preservation Foundation, and others.

**PHOEBE CUTLER** has written on a wide range of California landscape history topics, including *The Public Landscape of the New Deal* (1985). She received a National Endowment Award in 2002 and a Rome Prize in 1988. Cutler has an MLA from the UC Berkeley and a BA from Harvard.

**MARLEA GRAHAM** was always a gardener, but interest in garden history began with editorship of the Heritage Roses Group and intensified on becoming a founding member of CGLHS. She served as editor of *Eden* from 1997-2009.

Architectural historian **STEVEN KEYLON** is the past president of CGLHS and is the editor of the journal *Eden*. He is a founding member of the The Cultural Landscape Foundation's Stewardship Council and vice president of the Palm Springs Preservation Foundation.

**DAVID A. LAWS** is a historian, photographer, and travel writer. His work has appeared in numerous electronic and print media outlets, from the BBC and NPR to mobile apps, guidebooks, newspapers, magazines, and academic journals.

**H. RAY MCKNIGHT**, PhD, is a Professor Emeritus of English at California State University, Fresno, and holds degrees from Harvard and the University of North Carolina. From 2002 through 2012 he was chair of the Downtown Fresno Coalition.

**CHRISTINE EDSTROM O'HARA**, ASLA, is professor in landscape architecture at California Polytechnic State University, San Luis Obispo, and past president of CGLHS. She holds a BA from Stanford University, an MLA from University of Washington, and a PhD in Landscape Architecture from University of Edinburgh.

Overleaf: An abstract colonnade and regionally appropriate plants at Val Verde in Montecito.

**ANN SCHEID** holds an MA from the University of Chicago and a MDes from Harvard's Graduate School of Design. She has served as a Foreign Service Officer, a city planner in Pasadena, an architectural historian for the State of California, and the Curator of the Greene and Greene Archives.

**DESMOND SMITH** is a graduate of the University of Glasgow. After a career in industrial market research, he is now retired and living in Rhode Island. Having had the pleasure of playing both Pasatiempo and Cypress Point, he can attest to the splendor of both venues.

**LEE SOMERVILLE** is a garden historian and the author of *Vintage Wisconsin Gardens* and *A Place for Everyone*. She is co-President of the San Diego Floral Association and writes for *California Garden* magazine. Her interests include growing heirloom vegetables.

**DAVID C. STREATFIELD**, a founding member of CGLHS, is Professor Emeritus of the Landscape Architecture Department in the College of Built Environments at the University of Washington. A landscape historian, he authored the classic *California Gardens: Creating a New Eden* (1994). Over the years he has written, coauthored, edited, or otherwise contributed to approximately four dozen books and articles, and has received numerous awards. He also often serves as historian-consultant on landscape restoration projects.

**HAROLD TOKMAKIAN**, AICP, (1927-2016) retired after twenty-five years from California State University, Fresno, in 1992 as Professor Emeritus of Regional and City Planning. He held degrees from Stanford University with a BA and MA in architecture and Master of Regional Planning from Cornell University.

# ABOUT THE EDITORS

Coeditor **CHRISTINE EDSTROM O'HARA** is a professor of landscape architecture at Cal Poly, San Luis Obispo. She received her Bachelor of English from Stanford University, Master of Landscape Architecture from University of Washington, and PhD in Landscape Architecture from University of Edinburgh. In addition to teaching, Prof. O'Hara has had a landscape design practice for over twenty-five years. Within that practice, she consults on the restoration and preservation of historic landscapes by writing National Register nominations, Cultural Landscape Reports, as well as restoration and rehabilitation plans. She is the past president of the California Garden & Landscape History Society, trustee for the Olmsted Network, and is passionate about education and conservation of historic places.

Coeditor **SUSAN CHAMBERLIN**, ASLA, is a landscape historian and a licensed landscape architect with a degree in landscape architecture from the University of California, Berkeley and master's degree in architectural history from the University of California, Santa Barbara. She is a founding member of the California Garden & Landscape History Society and a former adjunct faculty member of Santa Barbara City College, where she taught garden history. In addition to contributions to *Shaping the American Landscape*, *Eden: Journal of the California Garden & Landscape History Society*, *Arts and Architecture* magazine, the journal *Site Lines*, historic structures reports, and other publications, she is the author of *Hedges, Screens & Espaliers* and was a contributing editor of several horticulture books.

# INDEX

## California Eden:
### Heritage Landscapes of the Golden State

By Christine Edstrom O'Hara and Susan Chamberlin

Copyright © 2024 California Garden & Landscape History Society, Christine Edstrom O'Hara, and Susan Chamberlin

Design by J. Eric Lynxwiler, Signpost Graphics

10 9 8 7 6 5 4 3 2 1

ISBN 978-1-62640-115-0

"Angel City Press" and the ACP logo are registered trademarks of Los Angeles Public Library The names and trademarks of products mentioned in this book are the property of their registered owners.

Library of Congress Cataloging-in-Publication Data is available

Published by Angel City Press at Los Angeles Public Library

www.angelcitypress.com

Printed in Canada

Overleaf: Starting with just a few species native to South America, there are now hundreds of varieties of bougainvillea.